THE BONANNO
MAFIA CRIME FAMILY

MAFIA LIBRARY

© **Copyright 2023 - All rights reserved.**

The content contained within this book may not be reproduced, duplicated or transmitted without direct written permission from the author or the publisher.

Under no circumstances will any blame or legal responsibility be held against the publisher, or author, for any damages, reparation, or monetary loss due to the information contained within this book, either directly or indirectly.

Legal Notice:

This book is copyright protected. It is only for personal use. You cannot amend, distribute, sell, use, quote or paraphrase any part, or the content within this book, without the consent of the author or publisher.

Disclaimer Notice:

Please note the information contained within this document is for educational and entertainment purposes only. All effort has been executed to present accurate, up to date, reliable, complete information. No warranties of any kind are declared or implied. Readers acknowledge that the author is not engaged in the rendering of legal, financial, medical or professional advice. The content within this book has been derived from various sources. Please consult a licensed professional before attempting any techniques outlined in this book.

By reading this document, the reader agrees that under no circumstances is the author responsible for any losses, direct or indirect, that are incurred as a result of the use of the information contained within this document, including, but not limited to, errors, omissions, or inaccuracies.

TABLE OF CONTENTS

Introduction 1

Chapter 1 : The Bonanno Family Origins 7
   Maranzano And American Prohibition 7

Chapter 2 : Joe Bananas And The Castellammarese War 13
   Joe Betrays The Boss 13
   The Fifth Family Of New York City 17

Chapter 3 : Ambition And Alliance 21
   Bonanno And The Mafia Commission 21
   1957: From Palermo To Apalachin 26

Chapter 4 : "He's Planting Flags All Over The World..." 33
   The Plot Against The Commission 33
   The Bonannos And The Sixth Family 37

Chapter 5 : The Banana Split 45

Chapter 6 : Philip Rastelli And The Civil War 53
   The Renegade 53
   Red Vs. Black 59
   Donnie Brasco 64

Chapter 7 : The New Massino Regime 73
    Aftermath: Brasco And The Mafia Commission Trial 73
    The Massino Family? 83

Chapter 8 : Massino, Mancuso, And The Mafia In The 2020s .. 95

Conclusion 109

References 113

INTRODUCTION

The year was 1981. A man known to his friends as Donnie Brasco had just entered the notorious Motion Lounge at 420 Graham Avenue in the Williamsburg neighborhood of Brooklyn, New York. Everyone in the area knew about Motion, and they stayed away if they didn't want trouble. Even to the New York Police Department, it was no secret that Williamsburg mobsters treated the lounge as their own personal crime headquarters. Donnie was known to the men inside. He wasn't a "made guy"—meaning he wasn't an official member of their Mafia Family—but he was well-connected and well-liked. Everyone greeted him, inquired about his illicit ventures, and life went on. But someone in the club was especially eager for Donnie's arrival. He stood up, called for him, and ushered him into a back room where illegal card games were often held. The two sat down, and the man opposite Donnie had an urgent, concerned look on his face. He was Dominick Napolitano, better known as "Sonny Black," and he was a notorious caporegime (captain) of the legendary Bonanno Mafia Crime Family. He had a job for Donnie.

Donnie was very happy that it was a job. Just a little while ago, he had stepped out of a plane fresh from Florida, where he conducted a lot of his business. While he was there, he got a call from a friend of his, a Bonanno soldier that he affectionately referred to simply as "Lefty" (soldiers are ranking members of a Family, below caporegimes). Lefty was in Sonny's crew, same as Donnie, and he often served as a go-between for the associate and captain. The message this time was that Donnie needed to get back to New York as soon as possible for a sit-down. Donnie knew there was plenty of strife in the family, betrayals and back-stabbings, so this could only mean one of two things: Either Donnie was needed for something very important, or he was marked for death. When he walked into the Motion Lounge that day, he still wasn't sure whether the men inside were planning on letting him walk out. Regardless, fleeing and going on the lam would have put him in an even worse position, so he showed up like a dutiful underling to hear the words of his captain.

Sonny Black pressed Donnie about his connections in Florida. He needed to know if they were reliable, capable, and willing to do some digging. Donnie answered in the affirmative, and so Sonny divulged his plan. He needed someone to go down to the Miami area, where a man known as Bruno was hiding. Donnie needed to kill him. Against the traditional code of the Mafia, the target was a member of Sonny's own Family, and, worse, he was the son of a made guy. Donnie assured him it wouldn't be a problem: "Sonny, you know me, I don't ask questions" (Pistone, 1989). It was a relief for Sonny. He had a lot of messes to clean up and a lot of wrongs to make right, but his problems were not even close to over. Earlier, the Williamsburg capo had orchestrated the execution of three captains of his own Family, one of them being Bruno's father. Some say it was a power-grab by Sonny, some say it was Sonny's attempt at preventing a power-grab. No matter how you looked at it, the Bonanno Family was clearly not in a great shape to start the new decade.

If Donnie could pull this off, though, maybe things would start to look up. At least for Sonny's crew, it would have been important. This hit would've been Donnie's first for the Family, and Sonny was planning on making him a made guy after it went through. But true to form, there was another problem, and it was a big one: Donnie Brasco was not real. The man that the Bonanno captain just gave execution orders to was, in fact, an undercover agent for the FBI, the first lawman to successfully infiltrate the American Mafia, and his name was Joseph D. Pistone. The "Donnie Brasco" persona he had crafted, based on his upbringing in mob-influenced New Jersey, had been fooling the Bonanno leadership since the late 1970s, with only a few higher-ups wary about his spotty backstory. The federal agent, of course, had no intention of carrying out "Sonny" Napolitano's orders. In fact, what he did instead would result in the execution or imprisonment of several high-ranking members of the Bonanno Family. Sonny, the man who welcomed Pistone/Brasco into his crew and vouched for his loyalty, was not spared the consequences.

The Donnie Brasco debacle was one of law enforcements crowning achievements in the war on organized crime, and it was one of the biggest embarrassments ever to plague a Mafia Family. The other four of New York's famous Five Families questioned how the Bonannos could have let something like this happen, and those within the Family questioned how they found themselves in such a state of distrust and betrayal. Why, on top of the FBI infiltration, was there so much internal strife among the Family ranks? How did one of the most respected and feared Families in the history of organized crime become reduced to infighting and civil wars, and how did they very nearly induct a federal agent into the highly secretive Mafia Family structure?

To understand how the Family found themselves in such dire straits by the 1980s, we must understand the history of the Bonannos, all the way back to before Joe Bonanno, the Family's namesake, was the big man in charge. The Bonannos were an old Sicilian family with roots in the Castellammare del Golfo (translated to "Sea Fortress on the Gulf") region of the island. Castellammare del Golfo always had significant Mafia presence, and in the early days of the Bonanno Family rule, their ranks consisted almost entirely of gangsters of Castellammarese origin. The regional backgrounds of the Bonannos and other Families would come to play later, in the 1930s, when the New York underworld nearly tore itself apart. As a young man, Joe Bonanno, later known by many as "Joe Bananas" or "Don Peppino," cut his teeth as a gangster working for Salvatore Maranzano, the chief of the Castellammarese clan in New York. Like most gangsters at the time, Bonanno was attracted to the criminal underworld because of the incredibly lucrative illegal alcohol market.

When alcohol was made illegal for manufacture and consumption in the US in 1920, very few people were planning on abiding by the law, and there were few jurisdictions in the country that cared enough to enforce it. On top of that, there were plenty of people willing to dabble on the wrong side of the law to make plenty of cash for a vice that many considered harmless. The manufacturing of liquor was relatively simple, if a bit dangerous, so homemade stills were set up across the country in major cities. In places like Chicago, Boston, Detroit, Buffalo, and, of course, New York City, it didn't take long for organized crime to dominate the underground market. The America Mafia was one of the chief players in the trade. With the experienced and old-school Maranzano as his mentor, Bonanno quickly became a rising star in the American crime scene. During the Castellammarese War that was to come in later years, Joe would also get valuable wartime experience that allowed him to rule his Family for years as one of the east coasts most feared bosses.

By the end of his tenure, Joe Bananas had been one of the longest-serving bosses in New York City, outliving the four other original bosses from the Castellammarese War. Known for his incredibly bold schemes and attempts to seize more power than one man should have, Bonanno left a personal legacy as complicated as that of the Family he created. Sometimes he was untouchable, sometimes he was valued as an advisor, and sometimes he was a pariah. Even after Don Peppino stepped aside as Family boss, the Bonanno Family history was a rollercoaster of betrayal, success, greed, and turmoil. They've had several falls from grace, and sometimes they've had their redemptions. Ultimately though, the mark that they have left (and continue to leave) on the American criminal underworld is a questionable one.

Through the chapters in this book, we will explore the complete complicated and contradictory history of the Bonanno Family, taking us through their earliest years up to the present day, from when they earned their reputation as the most brutal (and the most loyal) of New York's gangs to when they had themselves outcast from the Mafia structures almost entirely. Unlike the Genovese Family, for example, the Bonannos are not remembered for their successes, but rather for their self-destruction, isolationism, and tendency to "eat their own," a reputation which the Donnie Brasco incident did nothing to resolve. This is despite the fact that under Joe (and even some of his successors), the Family reached heights that other Families across the country could only dream of. Now, we will take a look at how it all played out.

CHAPTER 1
The Bonanno Family Origins

Giuseppe Carlo Bonanno, later Americanized as Joseph Charles Bonanno, was born on January 18, 1905, in Sicily, an island off the coast of southern Italy that many consider the birthplace of the Mafia. His hometown of Castellammare del Golfo was an especially Mafia-influenced region of Sicily—an entire branch of the American Mafia consisted of immigrants from this specific area. Joe's local roots would later characterize his organization in the US. His father, Salvatore Bonanno, was already involved in organized crime by the time Joe was brought into the world. Even his mother, Catherine Bonventre, came from a Family with a deep Mafia history in the region. In this kind of environment, it seems inevitable that Joe Bonanno would become involved in crime from a young age. Being both a Bonanno and Bonventre, Joe had no shortage of relatives from whom he could learn the trade. But his time in Sicily was short-lived. Not long after he was born, he and his family were on their way to start a new life in the US.

Maranzano And American Prohibition

When Joe Bonanno was just three years old, his father relocated the family to New York City. Like many Sicilian immigrants at the time, they eventually settled in Brooklyn. Along with Joe's family came several other Bonannos, as well as some Bonventres and Magaddinos. All of these families had histories in organized crime. Williamsburg, a neighborhood in Brooklyn, was a hotspot for Castellammarese immigrants, and this is where Joe eventually built his powerbase. Stefano Magaddino, another Castellammarese who had arrived in the US a few years earlier, was also in Brooklyn at the time. After Joe came to power, he and Magaddino would maintain a strong, close alliance for years, which increased both of their power. Stefano, much more experienced than Joe, had been allied with Bonannos since before they even left the old country. Unfortunately, Joe's ambition later led to the complete breakdown of this decades-old partnership.

In Williamsburg, the Bonannos carried on their small-time Mafia operations among their fellow immigrants, many of whom would have been used to the intimidation and extortion from the old country. But, after about a decade in the US, Salvatore decided to bring the family back to Sicily. Joe would have been leaving the country at about the same time as the outbreak of the bloody Mafia-Camorra war, which pitted the Sicilian Mafia factions against the Camorra factions, another criminal organization that originated in the Campania region of Italy—particularly Naples. Very little is known about Joe's time while he was back in Sicily, but by the time he returned to the US, the Mafia had emerged victorious over the Camorra and had established themselves as the premiere Italian organized crime group. It provided ample opportunity for the Sicilian Joe Bonanno, but at the time, the national Mafia structure was still highly fractured and rife with infighting.

While he was back in his Sicilian homeland, Joe steadily got more involved in organized crime. He was still very young, though, and he had several years before he would enter his prime. While on the island, two major factors motivated him to make his way back to America. First, in 1924, Italian dictator Benito Mussolini was two years into his reign of terror. Around this time, he began a brutal crackdown on Mafia operations on the island of Sicily and the southern Italian mainland. In general, Mussolini was successful in decimating Sicily's Mafia presence, and it subsequently became much harder for organized criminals to operate there. Meanwhile, on the other side of the Atlantic Ocean, American liquor prohibition was in full swing. The ban was four years old in 1924 and it had already become clear that the federal and local authorities were not willing to expend the effort to actually stop the consumption of alcohol. Nor, for that matter, were they really interested in prosecuting anyone who violated the law. So, the American bootleg liquor trade quickly became very lucrative and carried surprisingly few risks. In many counties of certain states, officers were told specifically not to waste resources making arrests for prohibition violations.

This was a very promising situation for Bonanno. Eventually, he decided he needed to get back to the US to get a piece of the action. The circumstances surrounding his journey are not well-known, but in 1924, he stowed away on a Cuban fishing vessel bound for the coast of Florida. How he managed this is a mystery, but it appears he made the journey along with Peter Magaddino, the son of Stefano. The pair slipped into the US while avoiding being detected by immigration services, which in 1924 were not nearly as robust as today. Their journey was, of course, illegal, meaning that

Joe had not even begun the process of becoming an American citizen. This would cause problems for him later, but he always managed to avoid being deported back to Sicily as some of his less lucky Mafia contemporaries had been.

Back in the US for the second time, Joe wasted no time at all. He quickly got involved in the liquor bootlegging business. His first known criminal enterprise was operating a homemade, jury-rigged liquor still in Brooklyn. For this, he teamed up with several other young immigrants also from Castellammare del Golfo. Local police were mostly a nonissue for Bonanno and his associates at the time. The worst that might have happened was a local cop might stroll in looking for a bribe, but the government in 1920 had established a branch called the Bureau of Prohibition, whose sole purpose was to prosecute and arrest those who smuggled, manufactured, purchased, or sold alcohol. Luckily for Joe and company, though, by 1924 the Bureau and its officers had become corrupt, bloated, overly bureaucratic, and terribly inefficient. Except for a few notable exceptions, like the infamous Eliot Ness, prohibition enforcement agents were notoriously easy to bribe or threaten, and many of them enjoyed indulging in illicit alcohol themselves. The reality was that, even if the Bureau was effective, there were simply too many people who wanted to drink and too many people willing to sell it to them.

Joe soon began working for the old-school Castellammarese gangster Salvatore Maranzano, who was involved in bootlegging, but also prostitution, illegal gambling, and drug trafficking. He reportedly used a semiphony real-estate company as his "front," which meant that his illegal income was funneled through the "legitimate" company in order to avoid suspicion from the Internal Revenue Service. Maranzano would have been arriving in the US around the same time that Bonanno was smuggling himself there, but Maranzano had much bigger connections than Joe. In fact, it's been alleged that Maranzano was in America in part on behalf of the powerful Don Vito Cascioferro (sometimes spelled Cascio Ferro, sometimes just Ferro), who was attempting to stretch his influence across the Atlantic into the Americas. Importantly, though, even if this is true, Maranzano would have had no intentions of handing over the reins or answering to Cascioferro, who was basically an entire world away. Still, Maranzano's mandate was clear: He was to seize control of the entire American Mafia structure. With Joe Bonanno quickly becoming a powerful enforcer for him, Maranzano would soon be prepared to wage war.

Business continued on nicely for several years, but everyone knew it wouldn't last. Eventually, many mobsters' greed and severely disorganized "Families" in New York City created friction between them. With no organized command structure, there was no one to cool tensions between the mob groups or quell the infighting. In 1930, things had reached a tipping point, and New York's Mafia crews were on the verge of a full-blown war. The match that lit the gas? Nothing more than some stolen liquor.

CHAPTER 2
Joe Bananas And The Castellammarese War

In 1928, the bad blood between the Castellammarese and the rest of the Sicilian factions exploded. For months, mobsters from both sides had been repeatedly hijacking each other's liquor trucks and selling them to competitors at a discount. Joe Bonanno's role put him right in the middle of this activity. He was one of the men that Maranzano had put in charge of organizing security for his booze shipments. As the Mafia edged closer to war, Bonanno was given even more power and responsibility. By the time the war broke out, in 1930, the young mafioso essentially functioned as Maranzano's wartime Commander-in-Chief, directing Castellammarese attacks on the other Sicilians.

Joe Betrays The Boss

In 1930, the non-Castellammarese faction of the Mafia was led by Giuseppe Masseria, nicknamed "Joe the Boss." Masseria was a native of Menfi, in Sicily, about 70 kilometers directly south of the Castellammarese homeland. In the old country, the two were practically neighbors, but in 1930 New York, those 70 kilometers meant all the difference. Masseria, who had been in the US for about two decades longer than either Joe Bonanno or Maranzano, was a formidable opponent with a multitude of connections in NYC. Masseria cut his teeth working for the legendary Giuseppe Morello, who was one of the first known mafioso to immigrate and take control of the NYC underworld. In short, Masseria was Mafia royalty. Still, status meant little in the Mafia when compared to greed and ambition.

Operating out of Brooklyn, the Castellammarese faction routinely traded blows with Masseria's crew. On the surface, the war was a conflict between Maranzano and Masseria, but there was also an underlying generational conflict—between the younger, more progressive mafiosi, some of whom were American-born, and the older, more traditional, and exclusively immigrant generation. These more conservative gangsters clung to so-called "old world" values, which the younger generation believed was an impediment to conducting business in America. For example, many of the older mafiosi at the time still refused to work with anyone who wasn't Italian. In most cases, even *being* Italian wasn't enough—they needed to be 100% full-blooded Sicilian or else the old-timers didn't trust them. The younger and more forward-thinking generation, which included Joe Bananas, realized that America was not Sicily. America was a diverse country where many different ethnic groups engaged in organized crime. Whereas those like Maranzano and Masseria would stick their noses up at them, the more modern gangsters realized that a lot more money could be made by working with Jewish, Irish, and African-American criminal groups. After all, Jewish gangsters of the time—including Dutch Schultz, Louis Lepke, and Meyer Lansky—were some of the biggest moneymakers in organized crime, and the younger generation of mafiosi were eager to partner in their schemes.

Eventually, a group emerged that came to be known as the "Young Turks." The loosely connected group was comprised of younger and more progressive gangsters from both Masseria's and Maranzano's factions. The group was led by the legendary Charles "Lucky" Luciano, who at the time was serving as Masseria's wartime lieutenant, but also included big names like Vito Genovese and Carlo Gambino from Masseria's side, as well as Stefano Magaddino, Joe Profaci, Tommy Lucchese, and, of course, Joe Bonanno himself, from Maranzano's side. The Young Turks were tired of the ongoing war, and they foresaw a future where the greed and egos of their bosses would lead to the destruction of the American Mafia before they even reached their prime. They needed to stop the infighting before the infighting stopped them.

Secretly, the cabal formed a plan. They agreed that the best course of action was to have Joe Masseria killed and allow Maranzano to emerge as the victor—at least for now. After a clandestine deal with the Castellammarese boss, the Young Turks arranged for a hit on Masseria, which was successfully carried out in April 1931, effectively bringing the war to an end. Unfortunately, after Masseria was gone, the Young Turks immediately became worried over Maranzano's apparent thirst for power. With Masseria gone, Maranzano bestowed upon himself the title of *capo di tutti capi,* or, in English, the "boss of all bosses." It was an old designation, originally held by Giuseppe Morello, but it didn't sit right with the younger gangsters, specifically Joe Bonanno. Worried that

Maranzano would soon become worse than Masseria had been, the Young Turks quickly turned on him as well.

While the Young Turks were scheming against Maranzano, it was revealed to Luciano and Bonanno that Maranzano, fearing treachery from Masseria's old crew, was also planning on killing them. After Lucchese told the other Young Turks that Maranzano had actually hired some hitmen, they knew it was time to act. In September 1931, just five months after the war ended, they quickly dispatched four Jewish gangsters to Maranzano's office. They disguised themselves as federal agents, which made it easy for them to disarm Maranzano's men, but when they reached his office, they didn't arrest him. Instead, they held him down and stabbed him multiple times before shooting him dead.

It has aways been a mystery whether Joe Bananas was complicit in the murder of his former mentor. He had always denied it, but he never sought any revenge for Maranzano's murder, and there is no evidence he was against the plan. Further, Bonanno benefitted greatly from Maranzano's removal, and he had no qualms about inheriting his crew. So, it's very likely that the murder was carried out with Bonanno's consent and blessing. Based on Bonanno's accounts, it seems that he wasn't confident that Maranzano would survive in the new generation, anyway. Despite being in the US for years by 1931, the "boss of all bosses" spoke shockingly little English, and all of his business had to be conducted in his native Italian. This made it very difficult for him to communicate with the newer, American-born generation of mobsters, and he very often required a bilingual translator. With Maranzano unwilling to change or adapt to the times, Joe knew that the situation wasn't sustainable with Maranzano at the helm.

The Fifth Family of New York City

The structure of the New York Mafia, which was organized into the famous "Five Families," was originally designed by Sal Maranzano, but it didn't take the shape we know today until after the Castellammarese War. After both old-timers were dead, Lucky Luciano was the *de facto* "boss of bosses"; however, he refused to officially adopt the title. Perhaps the most visionary mobster of his generation, he believed that the Mafia would be more peaceful and more prosperous without a single boss who controlled everything. As a result, he reorganized the Mafia into the more familiar structure that exists to this day. He created five distinct but connected Families, which would each have its own boss, and none of them would have jurisdiction over the others. The hope was that, instead of constant war and infighting, cooperation would be the new *modus operandi* of the Mafia. One of these new Families was given to Joe Bonanno, who inherited the vast majority of the remnants of Maranzano's former crew and businesses. As a result, the new Bonanno Family was almost exclusively Castellammarese.

This is where the Bonanno Family, as we know it, truly began: in 1931, with the official creation of the Five Families of New York City. At just 26 years old, Joe Bananas was easily the youngest of New York's bosses, which included Luciano, Tommy Gagliano, Vincent Mangano, and Joe Profaci. Despite his age and comparative lack of experience, Joe would eventually lead his Family to earning a reputation as the most ruthless and, as we'll see, ambitious Family in the state of New York. Unfortunately for the entire Mafia, prohibition was soon to be abolished and as a result, in 1933, the Mafia lost a massive portion of their income. American prohibition, which in many ways bankrolled and funded the first real iteration of organized crime, was done away with officially in early December of that year. Other avenues for cash were desperately needed, and like other Families, Joe got the Bonannos involved in multiple Mafia "staples," which included loansharking; prostitution (essentially pimping); extortion; narcotics trafficking; large heists; and illegal gambling rings, which included the infamous Italian "numbers" game (basically, an illegal lottery run by the Mafia that was popular in Italian neighborhoods).

Of course, Joe also had numerous semi-legitimate front businesses he used to launder the piles of illicit cash his Family was bringing in. These included several laundromats, a regional cheese distribution company that supplied the New York area (years later, a Canadian cheese company named Utica Cheese was also investigated for their connections to the Bonannos), and multiple coat factories. Through the years, Bonanno became active in New York City's garment district, and he was heavily involved with the International Ladies' Garment Workers Union (ILGWU, or just ILG), one of the largest labor unions in the nation at the time. Labor-union corruption very quickly became a lucrative moneymaking opportunity for the Bonannos and the other four Families. Most infamously, though, Joe also owned a funeral parlor in NYC and it was long suspected that the small shop was being used as a secret site for the Bonannos and their associates to dispose of dead bodies. According to most sources, they utilized specially made double-decker coffins in which their victim's body would be concealed in the lower deck while their clients' loved ones occupied the visible upper deck. It was an ingenious idea—no one would think to look in an already-occupied coffin, and if the law ever wanted to recover these bodies, they would have to exhume the remains of another corpse, which would no doubt have brought severe legal trouble from the deceased's living relatives.

Joe Bonanno's personal family life was also developing nicely in these early years. He soon settled down and had children with his new wife, Fay Labruzzo, whom he married just a couple months after inheriting the deceased Sal Maranzano's Family. Most notably, his first son was Salvatore Bonanno, nicknamed "Bill," who was born in 1932 and would go on to have a major impact on the Family. Fay also later gave birth to Catherine, their only daughter, and Joseph Bonanno, Junior. Despite not having yet seen his 30th birthday, Joe was clearly well-suited to run a Family. At the time, the Mafia leadership favored "wartime" dons—meaning those who had a proven track record of effective leadership through times of war. During the Castellammarese War, Joe served admirably and although he was technically a rival of Luciano at the time, he had clearly earned Luciano's respect. It also meant that Joe had seen the effects of war and the destruction that it brought, and someone like him would be more likely to avoid turning to conflict with the other Families (at least, that was the hope). Regardless, Joe was no stranger to getting his hands dirty and could be trusted to guide his Family through difficult, sometimes violent, times.

These early years defined Joe Bonanno as much as Joe Bonanno defined them. He was not yet the premiere Mafia boss in the nation—that position was occupied by Lucky Luciano—but his role was a vital one. This new era was centered around the leadership of

Luciano's Family, but Joe was instrumental in not only defining the new Mafia laws (like *omerta*, or the code of strict silence), but also in the creation of the national Mafia Commission, the brainchild of Luciano and his solution to the problems the Mafia was still facing in the early 1930s.

CHAPTER 3
Ambition And Alliance

In the new era of the New York City Mafia, it was pure ambition, drive, and key alliances that allowed the Bonannos to flourish. Even in peacetime, though, the Family would have competition, and the other bosses' greed could not be underestimated. In the Mafia world, as we'll see, even the strongest alliances are liable to break down, and betrayal was par for the course. This is where the Mafia Commission came in.

Bonanno And The Mafia Commission

Charles Luciano, a true criminal visionary, established the national Commission along with Joe Bonanno, in an attempt to prevent the Italian-American crime Families from once again tearing one another apart. Diplomacy, Luciano believed, was a preferable mode of business over backstabbing and violence. The Commission established democratic rule in the underworld, where recognized bosses would all have a say and decisions that affected more than one Family would be made by a committee of trusted members rather than the volition of a single man. Even hits within a Family would generally need approval by vote of Commission chairmen. Importantly, the Commission also replaced the need for a "boss of bosses," and, in fact, officially abolished the title completely. As an analogy, Luciano and Bonanno got rid of the dictator and installed a democratic electoral committee in his place.

Originally, Bananas and Lucky named the Commission "The Committee for Peace," which grants us a fair bit of insight into their original goals for the Commission. Hilariously, though, "Committee for Peace" in Italian (roughly, *Comitato per la Pace*) proved to be a bit of a mouthful, and younger American-born mafiosi who spoke only broken Italian apparently had tremendous difficulty pronouncing it (and vice versa—for those for whom Italian was their first language, the English translation was too complicated). In the interest of expediency and convenience, the two bosses quickly agreed to change the organizations name to, simply, The Commission, which could easily be pronounced in both languages (the Italian spelling was almost identical—*La Commissione*). Despite being a foundational member of The Commission, Joe Bonanno would, in his very long tenure as boss, run afoul with Commission chairmen several times.

One of the key purposes of The Commission was to regulate and limit membership, placing strict conditions for who could be "made." By placing these restrictions, The Commission hoped to restrict the growth of all of the Families to prevent any one Family or Families from massively growing their ranks and overpowering the other Families. In Mafia hits like *The Sopranos*, references are made to the "books" being open or closed—this is a reference to the Commission's real-life practice of allowing Families to recruit made men during some periods, and completely closing membership during others. In this way, The Commission served as a vital regulatory body. Needless to say, the American Mafia was becoming much more sophisticated and much more effective. These early Mafia innovations helped insulate organized crime from the national law enforcement, which at the time as lagging significantly behind the criminals they were supposed to be apprehending. But as we'll see, in later years, the Mafia stagnated, and while the FBI and New York state officials refined and reinvigorated their methods of going after and prosecuting organized crime, the Mafia rested on their laurels and became consumed by greed.

Unfortunately, and as several other bosses and their underlings feared, Joe eventually became much too ambitious for The Commission's liking, but this would only become a major problem in following decades. For now, everything seemed to be running smoothly. Joe began steadily increasing his influence and establishing important, lasting connections. He gradually and carefully began expanding his territory both within New York City and outside of the state. He cultivated early friendships with Families on the American west coast, particularly San Jose and San Francisco; in Buffalo, where his close friend and long-time ally Stefano Magaddino reigned supreme; and in Canada, with the help of Magaddino, who claimed the Toronto area and southern Ontario as his territorial jurisdiction. Toronto was a big and lucrative market that offered more than enough for Magaddino and Bonanno to share, but this would become a major thorn in the side of the Buffalo don, especially after Joe began making moves in Montreal, farther north.

After living in the US for decades, Joe Bonanno finally became a naturalized citizen in 1945, the last year of the Second World War.

Due to the fact that his 1924 entry was illegal, he was forced to head north and spend some time in Canada before re-entering the US legally so he could begin the naturalization process. Some speculated that he went to Canada to avoid the draft for WWII; others claimed that he was at no risk of being drafted because he wasn't a citizen yet. In reality, Bonanno was never at any real risk of being sent overseas to Europe or Asia, nor were any of the bosses of the Five Families at the time. While many subordinates in the Mafia participated in the war, including the Bonannos' own John "Johnny Green" Faraci, who is considered a hero of the 1944 D-Day landings in France, the bosses skated by without worry. As it turns out, their "legitimate" front businesses were the reason why. In America at the time, several industries were considered vital to the war effort, so the people who were key to running them were exempt. Bonanno's dairy and cheese company in New York was one of the industries considered necessary for the war. Plus Joe, like most other bosses, was heavily involved in national labor unions, which controlled the workforce of large manufacturing industries. With these tools in his pocket, Joe Bonanno was apparently considered too important to risk losing in a war. Joe was a criminal mastermind who had been gaming the government literally for decades, but as far as the military's draft rolls were concerned, he was just "a simple dairy farmer" (Sitwell, 2020).

Around the same time that Joe Bananas was working on getting his citizenship, he was forming an early and strong relationship with another of the original Five Family bosses—Joe Profaci. The Profaci Family, which was a forerunner to the Colombo Family (future boss Joe Colombo's father worked for Old Man Profaci at the time). The two bosses were perhaps the most close-knit out of any of the friendships on the Commission, and it was a very lucrative relationship (although these kinds of coalitions were technically frowned upon by Luciano). In 1956, their business and personal ties were taken to the next level when Sal "Bill" Bonanno, Joe's eldest, married Rosalie Marie Profaci, Joe Profaci's niece. It truly was a royal marriage of sorts, and it united two of the oldest Families in a way that ensured cooperation for years, at least up until Profaci's untimely death in 1962 from cancer. The Bonanno-Profaci wedding was a grand, momentous occasion for the Mafia underworld and was cause for celebration across the Five Families. It was so significant that film director Francis Ford Coppola, it's widely believed, used their wedding as a model for the famous opening wedding scene in *The Godfather*. The newlyweds held a grand reception at New York's ritzy Astor Hotel. Anyone who was anyone in the Mafia world was in attendance, and Tony Bennett even performed live for their guests (it's long been suspected that Bennett had Mafia ties, just like Frank Sinatra—in the film, Bennett was represented by the character Johnny Fontane, although his appearance was clearly styled after Sinatra). It was a sign of good times to come, but as we'll see, when the Profaci Family became the Colombo Family, long-standing ties simply can't last forever.

As the years went on, Bonanno became a trusted elder statesman figure among New York's organized criminals, and many mafiosi turned to him to settle disputes, even outside of his own Family. In the mid-1950s, Bonanno helped to cool tensions between boss Vito Genovese, who had inherited the Luciano Family, and Umberto "Albert" Anastasia, who headed Vincent Mangano's former Family, which would later morph into the Gambino Family. Bonanno was close to both of them, especially Anastasia, whom Joe supported in his bid to take over for Mangano in 1951 in the interest of avoiding another succession war. In Bonanno's 1983 memoir, *A Man of Honor,* Joe bathed in self-praise for settling the pair's dispute, awarding himself full credit for averting a gang war between the two Families. In retrospect, his boastfulness is hilarious considering that Anastasia was brutally murdered just a little while after, in 1957, under the direct order of Vito Genovese, paving the way for his friend Carlo Gambino to take over. Perhaps Joe Bananas didn't have as much sway as he thought he did.

1957: From Palermo To Apalachin

Aside from Anastasia's murder (and Joe's inability to quell the anger between Genovese and the deceased), 1957 proved to be a momentous year for the American Mafia, particularly the Bonanno Family. On the one hand, Mafia bosses were able to establish a lucrative, international deal that would define one of the main sources of the mob's income for decades to come, a deal that also (at least on paper) insulated American mafiosi from harsh legal penalties. On the other hand, 1957 very nearly saw the complete collapse of the American Mafia leadership structure. Both of these situations stemmed from seemingly benign meetings—one was back in the old country, the other was right in the Five Families' backyard. Both had massive implications for organized crime.

In October of that year, American Mafia elites, including Joe Bananas, flew across the Atlantic Ocean to pay a visit to the native homeland of their forefathers—the southern Italian island of Sicily. Specifically, they were destined for the capital city of Palermo, a breathtakingly beautiful coastal city on the northwestern edge of the small island. Sitting comfortably in the Gulf of Palermo abutting on the Tyrrhenian Sea, Palermo is a millennia-old city famed for its beautiful architecture (including its world-famous cathedral), but it is perhaps best known today for producing a huge proportion of American mobsters. Joe Profaci, Vincent Mangano, Carlo Gambino, Al Mineo, Joe "Iron Man" Ardizzone, and countless others hailed from Palermo or its surrounding areas. Even more American-born mobsters are able to trace their family lineage back to Palermo. To this day, the city's organized crime presence is considerable.

The delegation of American mafiosi that travelled to Palermo that fall included some of the biggest names in the US, but it was led primarily by Joe Bonanno, easily the most prominent of the attendees. The legendary Lucky Luciano was also in attendance, but he no longer represented the American Mafia and had been living in Sicily and Naples since he was deported from the US in 1946. In Bonanno's entourage were John Bonventre, widely believed to be Joe's underboss (second-in-command) at the time, as well as the up-and-coming Carmine Galante, who eventually became Joe's number-one narcotics man. Clearly, it was an important trip for the Bonanno Family. Dozens of other American and Sicilian mobsters attended.

According to Joe's published memoirs, the trip to Sicily was apparently a leisurely one. He flew across the Atlantic simply to visit his ancestral homeland, to take in the beautiful sights of southern Italy, indulge in some old-style Sicilian cuisine, and to visit friends and family from both the Bonanno and Bonventre clans. The Castellammarese don, however, fails to explain why he spent four consecutive nights at Palermo's luxurious Grand Hotel et des Palmes without taking a single trip into the countryside. The real reason, as it turned out, was to attend a meeting, held between October 10 and

October 14, to discuss and organize a transoceanic heroin deal between the American and Sicilian factions of the Mafia.

For months, Joe Bonanno and his Family had been stressing out over recent legislation passed in the US that was meant to curb and ultimately eliminate the flow of narcotics into the country. The incendiary *Boggs-Daniels Act*, which was passed in 1956, was especially concerning to Joe and the other Five Family bosses (at least those whose income, to a large degree, depended on peddling illegal drugs). *Boggs-Daniels* had a number of troubling clauses, but most importantly, it allowed for sentences of up to 40 *years* for drug offenses, plus it established mandatory minimum sentences for repeat offenders (for example, if the mandatory minimum is 10 years, those convicted will be sentenced for *at least* that amount of time, if not longer, regardless of how severe the offense was). Dealing drugs, which by this point was a staple of the Mafia stateside, was now a much riskier venture.

Joe Bonanno lamented at the passing of *Boggs-Daniels* and was openly concerned that the new, harsh penalties would make it far more enticing for his men on the street to rat or flip and turn state witness to save themselves from decades behind bars. He trusted that his top guys would not break the sacred *omerta* code of silence just to avoid a few years (some mobsters even went to prison for decades without ratting on their Families, sometimes for crimes they didn't even commit), but how might a younger, less principled mafioso react when faced with a potential 30 or 40 years in prison for pushing heroin? Joe had been complaining about the lack of integrity among American-born mobsters since at least the early '40s, and that was back when selling drugs was relatively easy. Now, he feared that one guy getting pinched on the street corner could topple the entire secrecy of the Mafia. This was his mindset going into Palermo in 1957.

There, in the Grand Hotel et des Palmes, a deal championed by Bonanno was brokered between the Five Families and the Sicilian factions. It would allow the old-country Families access to American territory for the first time since the end of the Castellammarese War in April 1931, more than 26 years ago. Under the groundbreaking Palermo deal, the Sicilians would be allowed to sell their products directly to distributors in Canada and the US. The American Families, in turn, would be paid by the Sicilian Families in exchange for access to their territory and for their official blessing to operate stateside. The connections that Bonanno had been cultivating in Canada became incredibly important in this new era—the so-called "French Connection" was vital to the new heroin deal, whereby the raw and refined heroin would travel through Turkey (opium poppies were grown in the Anatolia region and farther east) and into Sicily; from there it would either be processed or shipped into France to be processed. From France it would be smuggled into Canada through that country's eastern ports, and then finally it would be trafficked across the border into the US. Montreal, which would become a Bonanno stronghold, was a major hub for opiate smuggling. Needless to say, this ushered in a new age of drug smuggling, and after Palermo, the streets of America were flooded with heroin for decades.

About a month after Palermo, another important meeting took place—this time in Apalachin, a small community in Tioga County, New York. This meeting was important for a different reason, though. Vito Genovese, one of the five New York bosses, called the meeting to discuss various aspects of the Mafia underworld and to go over certain developments in terms of law enforcement. In reality, though, Genovese called the meeting to make his long-awaited grandstand in which he hoped to assert his status as the top dog in the New York criminal world. Essentially, he wanted to become a kind of pseudo-"boss of bosses." After the successful hit on Albert Anastasia a month earlier, Genovese felt that he was destined to be the number-one don in the country, and here, at the home of Joe "The Barber" Barbera (who was the boss of another Family based out of Pennsylvania), on November 14, 1957, he intended for all the other bosses to acknowledge it.

Large meetings between Mafia heads like this were not at all uncommon, but they were generally smart about it. The meetings were typically held at least four months apart and in a different location each time so as to avoid wiretaps or bugs by law enforcement. This time, though, Genovese insisted that the meeting be held just one month after the last one, in the same house, in the same small town. Joe Bonanno, often the voice of reason in situations like this, warned both Genovese and his close friend Stefano Magaddino that it was a terrible idea and that they would be asking for trouble. Magaddino agreed, but Genovese wouldn't hear it—the meeting went through anyway. In the Genovese boss's mind, he needed a large gathering as soon as possible after Anastasia's death in order to consolidate his power and to let everyone know what he planned on doing to those that opposed him.

Unfortunately for Genovese, the meeting was an abortive failure and Bonanno was proven correct. Local police caught wind that something big was happening well before the national Mafia representatives even landed in New York City. Apparently, they were tipped off by a large number of suspicious hotel reservations, which were all scheduled for the same time and registered to a single person who was known to be involved with the New York mob. When Apalachin eventually took place, New York police were already on alert. After noticing the huge number of luxury cars all parked at Barbera's large manor, many with out-of-state plates, local cops began taking down license-plate numbers and were eventually given the go-ahead to raid the home.

While Genovese was making his display of power and grandeur inside the house in front of Bonanno and the other skeptical bosses, police burst into the home and began arresting everyone inside. Panicked, many of the mobsters in attendance, dressed in fancy suits and wearing expensive jewelry, fled through whatever exit they could find and began trying to flee on foot. Almost all of them were apprehended quickly, including Joe Bonanno, who was hilariously caught and identified while he was trudging and stumbling his way through a cornfield behind the Barbera home. Later, Bonanno claimed that he wasn't even at the Apalachin meeting and that, in fact, his driver was the one who was caught and was mistakenly identified as Joseph C. Bonanno by police because he was carrying Bonanno's license on his person. This is a particularly hilarious explanation, considering that Joe Bonanno's personal driver would have no reason to be at the Barbera residence if Joe wasn't in attendance, and he also wouldn't need to be carrying Joe's identification. More likely, the man was eager to protect his opulent reputation and didn't want to admit that he had to resort to fleeing from the police on foot through the dirt in his designer shoes.

Of all the mobsters arrested at Apalachin in 1957, exactly zero convictions came as a result. There simply wasn't anything concrete to pin on the attendees, including Joe Bananas, who by this time was also sometimes known as "Don Peppino." Nearly all the mobsters present claimed that they were simply visiting Barbera, a friend of theirs, who had been sick for some time. It was a terribly unconvincing lie, considering that dozens of them had showed up at the exact same time, some having flown in from as far away as California, Missouri, Colorado, and Texas, but it was apparently enough to secure their freedom. Still, it was a dark day for the Mafia. For decades, the Mafia had maintained an air of mystery, largely due to the fact that its members were forbidden from acknowledging its existence to *anyone* outside the Families. Although most of the American public had a vague idea of what the Mafia was, and a general understanding that some kind of Italian-American organized crime organization existed, its extent was still largely uncertain. Unfortunately for the mafia, after the huge bust at Apalachin made national headline news, no mobster could convincingly deny that some kind of organized-crime network existed, and if they did, neither the American people nor government prosecutors would take them seriously. The details of the Mafia were still a secret, but that too was soon to come to an end. Ultimately, the Bonanno Family got off easy after Apalachin—it was the rival boss Vito Genovese that took the fall for its failure—but the fact that he had been exposed at such a high-profile event was bad news for his Family's future.

CHAPTER 4
"He's Planting Flags All Over The World..."

Throughout the 1950s, Joe Bonanno managed to remain mostly untouchable, but most of his fellow Five Family bosses had no such luck. Luciano was long since gone, and Tommy Gagliano and Vincent Mangano both died in the first years of the decade. By the early 1960s, only Joe Bonanno and his close ally, Joe Profaci, remained. This alliance, too, was not going to survive forever. The '60s was an era that posed serious problems for both Joe and his Family; his reputation as a calm and peaceful arbiter of Mafia justice was soon to be shattered completely. His obvious greed, thirst for power, and aggressive expansionism became too much for the new generation of the Mafia to accept.

The Plot Against the Commission

In 1961, the Bonanno-allied Profaci Family was facing its first of a series of deadly and violent internal conflicts. Joe Gallo, a notoriously unstable (and, as was discovered later, very likely schizophrenic) made man in the Family, had kidnapped four other high-ranking Profaci men, including his the boss' brother Frank, in a bid to seize power. The result is known as the First Colombo War, and it threatened to unseat Joe Bonanno's only real ally in New York City. On top of this, Profaci was battling cancer, and after several of his close friends advised him to retire for his own health, he died in 1962.

Joe Bonanno was now perhaps the most vulnerable he had ever been. He was now the last of the original Commission-era bosses still running a Family in NYC, and aside from Magaddino in Buffalo, Joe was isolated. Despite the fact that Joe was more progressive and forward-looking than the majority of his generation of made guys, he was still viewed with contempt by some of the younger mafiosi, both within and outside the Family. Further complicating Joe's position, a new alliance had formed after Profaci's death between Tommy Lucchese, boss of Gagliano's former Family since 1951, and Joe Colombo, a high-ranking member of the now-bossless Profaci Family. Together, this alliance could potentially threaten the powerful Bonanno Family. If Bonanno was to continue his ascent within the New York criminal underworld, he would need to take action to prevent himself from becoming a victim of his fellow bosses' greed.

There was another major problem that faced the entire Mafia in the first half of the '60s: Back in 1959, a made guy in the Genovese Family, a soldier named Joe Valachi, was arrested and charged with narcotics trafficking, and ultimately was sentenced to 15 years in prison. Convinced that Vito Genovese had marked Valachi for death, the soldier approached the government while incarcerated and offered to trade information in exchange for protection and a possible reduction in his sentence. A deal was struck and the traitor Valachi took the stand in 1963 in what became known as the

Valachi Hearings, overseen by Senator John McClellan from Arkansas. Valachi was planning to spill information about the Mafia that had been kept secret for decades. When it came time for him to speak, he detailed information not only about the current state of the Five Families, but also their histories. He named the original five bosses as well as the current bosses. He even detailed the "sacred rites" of the Mafia induction ceremony, which included bloodletting and holding a picture of a saint in the palm of the hand as it's lit on fire. Valachi became the first made man in history to publicly admit the existence of the Mafia, and he had confirmed what many suspected for a long time: It was the most flagrant violation of *omerta* in the Mafia's history. Most importantly for our story, Joe Bonanno was named personally by the now-infamous Genovese turncoat.

Soon after Profaci died, control of the Family was seized by Joseph "Evil Eye" Magliocco, a union racketeer and gifted chef. Generally speaking, Magliocco was viewed as a rather weak leader by most of his fellow Profaci men, but more troubling was the fact that his rise to power was not endorsed by the Mafia Commission. Despite this, Joe Bonanno openly supported Magliocco and assisted him in consolidating his base of power, in direct contradiction to the unofficial Commission rules. Aware that the other bosses likely wouldn't continue to tolerate his flagrant attempt at power grabs, Bonanno decided to act first. Together with his new (though far weaker) ally Magliocco, Bonanno crafted a violent, audacious, and completely unprecedented plot against the Mafia Commission. Their plan was to orchestrate several assassinations of Commission chairmen, including Lucchese, Gambino, and even Stefano Magaddino, in Buffalo. Magaddino, who had once helped Bonanno branch into Canada, had since grown resentful toward his fellow Castellammarese boss for his blatant power grabs and attempts to muscle him out of his own territory in Toronto. Plus, Bonanno had also expanded his connections farther north into Montreal, Quebec, the city where a massive portion of the Mafia's heroin was channeled. Magaddino reportedly complained that Joe was "planting flags all over the world," and believed he was becoming too ambitious for his own good. Joe knew that Magaddino felt this way, and so forsook their long-standing alliance, likely in attempt to muscle into Upstate New York, as well.

Bonanno had several other targets as in cities across the US, including California. Magliocco, for his part, offered to take care of the targets in NYC. This is where mistakes were made. Magliocco decided to give the contracts to the ambitious and up-and-coming made guy named Joe Colombo. Unfortunately for Bonanno and Magliocco, Colombo was apparently a more honorable, less obedient man than they had assumed. Colombo was unwilling to break Mafia code by carrying out obviously unsanctioned hits on fellow made men, let alone Family bosses like Lucchese and Carlo Gambino. He had his own idea—instead of planning the hits, Colombo had a sit-down with the chairmen of the Commission and explained to them, step-by-step, exactly what Profaci's unendorsed successor had told him to do.

The members of the Commission were appalled, but perhaps not exactly *surprised* by the news. After all, Magliocco knew that his position was tenuous at best and that he had made more than a few enemies on the Commission by his little stunt. But the Commission also knew that Magliocco was not powerful enough, and likely not clever enough, to organize a plot like this on his own. Plus, with only a portion of Profaci's old Family supporting him and the entire Joe Gallo faction still at war, Magliocco was not nearly powerful enough to deal with the inevitable backlash that would result from the hits if they were successful. Naturally, they suspected Joe Bonanno, the resentful veteran of the old school who believed he had a right to dominate the Commission. Infuriated, the Commission leadership summoned both co-conspirators to explain themselves, but Bonanno never showed his face. He had connections all over and would be able to find shelter in most large cities where the Mafia operated. So, he decided to go on the lam. Magliocco, who did not have close to the same national power that Bonanno did, had little choice but to face the consequences. He attended the sit-down with the Commission, with his tail between his legs and begging for forgiveness, explaining that Bonanno was the true mastermind behind it all. Given his advanced age and the Commission's desire to avoid further bloodshed of made men, they decided to show mercy to the former Profaci captain. He was forced to retire from the Mafia completely, and Joe Colombo, the man who ratted on the pair of schemers, was rewarded with total control of the Family.

The Bonannos And The Sixth Family

By the time Joe Bonanno and Joe Magliocco's plot against the Commission came to light, the Bonanno Family had extended its tentacles far and wide—they had gone interstate and international. Joe had especially strong connections in Arizona and in both San Jose and San Francisco in California. He also had mafiosi that reported to him in upstate New York (Magaddino's territory), as well as Wisconsin and Colorado. Outside of the country, Joe had close familial ties to the old Sicilian Families, especially in his native Castellammare del Golfo. Montreal was firmly in Bonanno's iron grip; his men there had also been making inroads in Toronto and Hamilton, the vital steel-producing port town in southern Ontario. After the Palermo Meeting in the '50s, Joe Bonanno personally endorsed the powerful Calabrian boss in Montreal, Vincenzo "Vic" Controni, and assigned him to oversee Bonanno interests in the northern city. Technically, Cotroni wasn't Mafia, but rather "*Ndrangheta*, another kind of Italian criminal organization whose roots are traced to Calabria rather than the island of Sicily. Luigi Greco, a Sicilian, was selected to be Cotroni's second-in-command in Montreal. Both of these men, despite owning their own territory, reported directly to Joe Bananno.

Vic Cotroni worked very closely with Carmine Galante, the top Bonanno narcotics guy, who first went to Montreal in the early '50s to coordinate the Family's interests in the heroin smuggling trade. Gerlando Sciascia, affectionately known as "George from Canada," served as the Bonanno liaison between New York City and Montreal, since he had close ties to both cities (he originally migrated to Montreal in 1955 and relocated to NYC a few years later, but maintained his connections to the Cotronis in Canada). With the full support of the powerful Bonanno Family, the Cotronis were able to rise above all of their considerable competition and maintain peace in Montreal for years—they grew incredibly powerful as a result. The Cotronis soon came to be regarded as the "Sixth Family," in reference to NYC's Five Families, but that title was eventually granted to a different Montreal faction, the Sicilians led by notorious mobster Nicolo Rizzuto. For the time being, though, the Cotronis were the ones that ensured massive drug profits for the New York clan.

This arrangement faced significant turmoil after the failure of Joe's outrageous plot against the commission. Whereas the chain of command was clear in the '50s, and Joe personally guaranteed stability in both Canada and the several American states where the operated, after Colombo exposed the plot, Joe completely disappeared. Even high-ranking members of his own Family had no clue where the don had gone. It's possible that his son Bill had a vague notion of his whereabouts, but as we'll see, the younger Bonanno had problems of his own to deal with. But the bottom line was that Joe had plenty of reasons to flee NYC. Obviously, the Commission and the rest of the Five Families were after him for what he had planned to do to them. Joe likely wouldn't have been killed, at least not right away, because the Commission did not want to set a precedent of ordering a hit on a fellow Commission chairman (which, for the time being, Joe still was), but Joe was still despised and was effectively a Mafia pariah. Plus, the other bosses feared a potential mob war emanating from the out-of-state regions where Joe held significant power, particularly Arizona and Canada. Even if they didn't order his death, the Commission certainly would have demanded monetary reparations, the surrender of all of Bonanno's business interests, and forced him to retire. Any of these scenarios were unacceptable to the ambitious boss.

On top of all of this, in October 1964 Joe was ordered to appear before a New York Grand Jury to answer questions and testify about his alleged illegal racketeering operations. With both the federal and state governments after him, and several New York wise guys calling for his head, it was completely unsurprising that Don Peppino disappeared without a trace. The last time he was seen in New York was actually the night before he was set to appear in court, which was awfully convenient timing. But much later, Joe also had a convenient excuse that he gave to the government for why he failed to show up. According to the Bonanno boss, he had every intention of showing up to his hearing, but he was supposedly kidnapped by rival mafiosi under the orders of the Mafia Commission (though Joe, of course, did not mention the existence of the Mafia or the Commission explicitly). In his memoir, Joe alleges that he was forced into a car by gunmen the night before while he was preparing for his court appearance. He was then driven to a remote location in the Catskills, a mountain range in Greene County, New York, about 120 miles north of Manhattan. There, Joe was faced by members of the Commission and their hired guns, who demanded an explanation for the plot and sought Bonanno's cooperation in cooling the tensions in New York that had flared up in the wake of its failure.

Whether or not the kidnapping was true (many people, even at the time, were very skeptical), Joe did eventually get into contact with the Commission. The Five Families' leadership wanted him to step down from his position and resign peacefully, although in disgrace. Joe apparently agreed, but under one condition: his son Salvatore "Bill" Bonanno was to be given full control of his former Family after the elder Bonanno was out of the picture. This, perhaps unsurprisingly, was unacceptable to the rest of the New York bosses, who believed that Bill would be too ambitious like his father, and that keeping another Bonanno around would cause bad blood both within and outside the Family. In their eyes, Joe had surrendered the right to back his son as his heir the moment he decided to break Commission rules and move against Lucchese, Magaddino, Gambino, and the others. Plus, they had no way of guaranteeing that Joe would not simply use his son as a puppet and continue to run the Family by proxy through Bill. So, the Commission categorically denied this condition, believing that Joe was in no position to negotiate a deal, anyway.

Instead, they supported a relatively unknown Bonanno soldier, an old-timer named Gaspare DiGregorio, for the position of boss. DiGregorio had certainly been around a long time, and got his start during prohibition, something fewer and fewer mobsters these days could claim. He had lived through the bloody Castellammarese War, which he'd fought alongside Joe Bonanno, Lucky Luciano, and other big names. Though he didn't have nearly the reputation that his contemporaries had earned by this time, DiGregorio commanded, if nothing else, respect. He was held in the same esteem that a soldier in Vietnam may have held for a veteran of World War II. He was certainly well-suited to at least be a powerful figurehead, and this spelled trouble for Bonanno. To complicate the matter even further, DiGregorio had apparently been quite close to Joe Bonanno and his Family for a long time. Back when DiGregorio still had ambitions of becoming *consigliere* someday, he was becoming well-connected and well-liked within Joe's circles. Years ago, after first coming to the US, DiGregorio had married the sister of Stefano Magaddino, the boss of the Buffalo Family and relative of Joe Bonanno. He also had a close personal friendship with Joe dating back years—he was the best man at Bonanno's 1931 wedding to Fay Labruzzo. He was even named godfather to Joe's first son, Bill, the same man he was now vying with for control of the Family.

Despite the familial relations to his opponent and the fact that he was backed by just about everyone else, Bill continued to press his claim to the throne. This course of action soon split the once-united Bonanno Family down the middle, and as we'll see, it had deadly consequences.

It's unclear exactly how Joe escaped his captors in the Catskills unscathed, if it actually happened at all, but Joe was missing for about two years, regardless. The best evidence suggests that Joe initially fled to California, probably to San Francisco, where he would have ample protection. From there, he found himself in Canada, where he remained until eventually returning to New York. While there, he was very likely under the protection of the Cotroni Family. But even here, things were beginning to get shaken up. Luigi Greco, Vic Cotroni's number two, had formed a clandestine alliance with the ambitious up-and-comer Nicolo Rizzuto, who had just migrated to Canada in 1954 and maintained powerful ties to the Sicilian Families. This posed a potential threat to Joe's power base in Canada. To shore up support for the Bonanno faction, Joe and Cotroni arranged to bring extra muscle into Montreal to offset the Greco-Rizzuto faction. The man they brought was Paolo Violi, yet another rising star who was a member of the powerful Magaddino-allied Luppino Family, which dominated Hamilton, Ontario.

Violi agreed and left Hamilton for Montreal, where he quickly became Cotroni's top captain. Magaddino was incensed—as if plotting to kill the Buffalo boss wasn't enough, now Joe Bonanno was poaching one of his top guys north of the border. Needless to say, relations between the two Castellammarese bosses were permanently destroyed. For a time, things remained peaceful for the Bonannos' Montreal faction, but things would boil over in the coming years, when the renegade Sicilian faction, led by Nicolo Rizzuto, went to war. Some of Joe's key supporters in Canada would end up dead, and the Cotroni Family was eventually supplanted by the Rizzuto Family, who took on the mantle of "Sixth Family." Before this happened, though, the core Bonanno Family in New York City was preparing to tear itself apart, all thanks to the power vacuum left behind when Joe went on the lam.

CHAPTER 5
The Banana Split

After Joe Bonanno fled New York, his Family was left in disarray. Without the boss present to keep everyone under control, the Family split into two opposing factions: the first was composed of those who supported Bill Bonanno's claim to power (i.e., those who were still loyal to Joe and wanted to maintain a sense of continuity between bosses); the other was led by those who supported the Commission-appointed Gaspare DiGregorio. These mafiosi were already displeased with Joe, sick of his constant absenteeism and his latest decision to abandon the Family. Many felt personally betrayed by Joe and thought that his underhanded plot to seize control of the Commission needlessly and selfishly put them all in danger and potentially ruined their ability to cooperate with the other NYC Families. Moreover, most of DiGregorio's supporters believed that Bill's attempt to seize control was an obvious case of Mafia nepotism and that the younger Bonanno had not "earned his stripes." It was not uncommon for sons of bosses to inherit their father's position, but in Bill's case, a good portion of the Family believed he was unfit to rule a whole organization. This was also true for Carlo Gambino and Tommy Lucchese, who also believed Bill had no right to rise to the same position as them. He would have been nothing without his father, and unlike Bill, Gambino and Lucchese had to work to earn their positions.

Joe's departure was obviously distressing to Bill. His father, the boss, had left him alone to deal with the mess in New York City that he'd created, and before doing that, he had ruined the reputation and standing of the Bonannos in the eyes of both their enemies and their allies. During the strife that followed, Bill could have, perhaps, turned to his father's old friends for guidance, men like Profaci, Magaddino in Buffalo, or Magliocco, but they were all either dead or had turned against Joe Bonanno and his Family. Bill was left utterly alone aside from the few made guys that still backed his father, wherever he was. To make matters worse, the FBI had an informant on the inside reporting on the activities of the Family for nearly the entire duration of the conflict. The FBI maintained an unusually high level of intel on what was going on, including profiles of which gangsters supported whom and what was going down at what time. The fact that the FBI seemed to always be a step ahead may have been an even greater cause for concern for Bill—but there is reason to believe that the informant in question was actually Bill Bonanno himself. Details of the FBI's profile in their unnamed informant explain the trepidation of the informant and his conflicted mental state, which began right around the time Joe Bonanno disappeared from NYC. Later reports detail that the informant abruptly became unwilling to cooperate, and this aligned perfectly with Joe's surprise reappearance in the city. Plus, more information appeared to be known about Bill's opposition mobsters rather than his own supporters. If this was the case, it's likely that Bill was both seeking a safety net, should the conflict turn against him, and was also using the FBI as a tool to covertly weaken

DiGregorio's faction. The true identity of the informant may never be known, but it seems likely that Bonanno Junior was working for the government, at least temporarily.

Although the two factions were clearly at odds, there was relatively little violence in the beginning. The Bonanno Family were already in the Commission's bad graces, and neither Bill nor DiGregorio wanted to be the one that initiated another deadly and costly gang war, which would only further ruin their reputation. Ironically, the first real instance of violence occurred at a supposed "peace meeting" that was meant to quell the tensions and work out a solution to the dispute in leadership. In January 1966, DiGregorio contacted Bill and his supporters to arrange a sit-down. As was often the case in situations like these, the man who offered the sit-down allowed the recipient to choose the location of the meeting to put them at ease and erase any suspicions they might have that they were being lured into a trap. Bill chose the home of a relative who lived out in Brooklyn, and DiGregorio agreed. Unfortunately for Bill, his concerns were valid—DiGregorio had no intention of meeting with Bill and planned to take him out before he even set foot in his uncle's home. While Bill and his men were approaching the meeting site, hitmen from DiGregorio's faction were lying in wait outside. As he walked up the property, they opened fire on Bill with machine guns. Bill's men hastily pulled out their guns and fired back, but the shooters quickly drove off after failing to put down the young Bonanno. Surprisingly, no one on either side was killed or even injured, but this little incident only led to more violence. The two sides were now engaged in open conflict.

While this was playing out, Joe was still MIA, evading both mafiosi, who wanted him dead and federal agents who wanted to see him behind bars. He was the only boss at the time who would have been a realistic target for the new anti-racketeering laws, which were championed by Robert F. Kennedy, the U.S. attorney general who later became a New York Senator, and brother of recently slain president John F. Kennedy. Amazingly, even with all this heat on him, Joe didn't stop his scheming while he was on the run. While in California, he was continuing his attempt to dominate the national Mafia scene, and he had his eyes set on Los Angeles, home of the Los Angeles Crime Family headed by Frank DeSimone, son of the venerable Rosario DeSimone. Frank was one of Joe's targets in the Commission plot, the exposure of which actually turned the LA boss into a neurotic paranoid, and Joe figured he may as well try to finish the job while he was out there. Joe had long viewed DeSimone as a weak leader who was either unable or unwilling to capitalize on the absolutely massive criminal market that a city like Los Angeles, which dwarfed both San Francisco and San Jose in size, had to offer. If Joe could somehow unseat DeSimone and allow Bill to move in, the Bonannos would be able to control all of California from their bases in SF, SJ, and LA. Then, assuming the Family could regain control back in NYC, the Bonanno Family would control Mafia operations on both the east and west coasts.

It's unknown exactly what Joe did to serve these goals, but he clearly failed. Frank DeSimone had become a difficult person to get a hold of, secluding himself after the Commission plot, and so Joe would have had his work cut out for him. Back in New York, Commission leaders were growing displeased with DiGregorio's failure to stop the infighting and bring the two Bonanno factions under control.

As a result, the Bonanno Family officially lost their Commission representation—they were still technically a part of the national organization, but the boss no longer had a seat at the table, nor could they vote on important national Mafia matters. Then, in 1968, there was a successful hit on several of DiGregorio's men, and the boss himself was wounded in a hail of machine-gun fire. Soon after, DiGregorio had a serious heart attack, likely as a result of the stress of the gang war, and he had no choice but to retire. Just two years later, DiGregorio died from lung cancer. After he stepped down, the Commission shifted their support to Paul Sciacca, the guy that most of Bonanno's men suspected of leading the failed hit on Bill back in early 1966.

By 1968, both factions had suffered significant losses in what the New York media had taken to calling the "Banana War," or, more cleverly, the "Banana Split." There was still no clear path to Joe returning as New York's premier crime boss, and it seemed that the Gambinos, Luccheses, and Colombos would not stop supporting his and Bill's enemies anytime soon. Joe had briefly resurfaced in 1966, finally reporting to the authorities and claiming that his kidnapping was the reason he had failed to report to them two years prior. No one, including the Feds and even his own guys, bought his story—most of them believed that he had simply abandoned them. In this context, the legendary Don Peppino finally agreed to abdicate from Mafia operations and leave New York City permanently, relinquishing all of his property and businesses there. He retired to a supposedly quiet life in Tucson, Arizona. Without Joe, Bill had essentially no claim to power; it was only a matter of time before what remained of his support began to crumble and fall away. Sciacca was more capable than DiGregorio, anyway, and likely would have siphoned support away from Bill as his men grew tired of the bloodshed. So, at the prodding of the other bosses, Bill retired as well, moving to San Jose, California. Both father and son were threatened with immediate death if they showed their faces in New York again. The pair of them were meant to essentially live as civilians for the rest of their lives, but it seems quite likely that they both stayed involved in small-time crimes considering each moved to a city where Joe had extensive influence and lucrative side operations.

So it was that Joe Bonanno, the longest-serving of the original Five Family bosses, was removed in disgrace from the Mafia, whose structure he helped create back in the 1930s. This was a man who witnessed some of the largest Mafia wars in history and survived through them by the skin of his teeth. He had made his bones during American prohibition, and when that was no longer an avenue for profit, he helped usher in a new era of narcotics that flooded America's streets with illicit drugs controlled by La Cosa Nostra. Needless to say, it was the end of an era. In the end, it was his audacity, greed, and delusions of grandeur that led to his demise. He was lucky enough to make it out of the Mafia alive, but his legacy was forever tarnished, especially after he chose to pen a supposedly tell-all book about his experiences later in his life. Though it was filled with lies, embellishments, and exaggerations meant to prop up his legacy and to massage his own ego, it was still taboo for a boss, of all people, to admit that he was part of the secretive Mafia organization and to profit off spilling other mobsters' secrets. To this day, the Family he once led is still known by his name, a testament to the mark he left on the underworlds of New York,

Montreal, California, and elsewhere. The age of Joe Bananas was in the rearview mirror by the time the 1970s rolled around.

So, the 1960s ended technically in a state of peace, although significant and likely irreparable damage was done to the Family. There were still tensions between various factions, and the Bonannos had lost their power from the Commission. They were pariahs and they knew it would take years, possibly decades, until they were back in the good graces of the national crime syndicate. The once-respected Bonanno Family now had questionable leadership and there was more than one made guy who believed he deserved to run the show. The "Banana Split" war was over, but it would not be the last time the Family tried to tear itself apart, and the coming decades had more than one tragedy in store for them. The Bonannos would never return to their glory days.

CHAPTER 6
Philip Rastelli And The Civil War

Short-term bosses. Back-stabbings. Civil wars. Rats, informants, and wiretaps. This was the future of the Bonanno Family that Joe Bananas left behind when he went to live out his days in sunny Tucson, never having to deal with the repercussions of his actions. Desperate attempts were made to once again unite the Family into something resembling the Bonannos of the 1950s, but to no avail. With each passing year, things only seemed to get worse, and none of the next few bosses stuck around long enough to provide a sense of stability. There was still a lot of bad blood from the Banana Split, and folks like Carmine Galante, Sonny Black, and a gentleman known as Donnie Brasco did nothing but throw gasoline on the still-burning embers.

The Renegade

To his credit, once the war was over, the new Commission-backed boss Paul Sciacca attempted to treat old wounds. He extended the olive branch by promoting members from the different Bonanno factions to positions of power to calm and appease the warring gangsters. Natale Evola, the man who was the current *de facto* boss of the faction that supported Joe and Bill Bonanno, was made Sciacca's underboss. Evola, another mobster of Castellammarese descent, was one of Bonanno's narcotics guys who worked closely with the loose cannon Carmine Galante, and was recently released from prison after being sentenced to a 10-year bid in 1959 for drug-smuggling charges. Philip "Rusty" Rastelli, a slightly younger and more influential mafioso whose loyalties were a bit more ambiguous, was made Sciacca's consigliere. Rastelli had been building up a rather robust base of power among the younger made guys as well as the associates of the various Bonanno crews.

Sciacca did an admirable job trying to repair the broken Family, but his efforts were ultimately in vain. Besides, he didn't have much time left as boss to continue making a difference. In 1970, Sciacca only would have been about 61 years old, but already his health was taking a turn for the worse, which wasn't aided by the additional stress of being the hastily thrown-in boss of a crumbling Mafia structure. On top of this, he was currently under investigation for serious crimes related to heroin trafficking. By the end of 1970, he had effectively stepped down as boss, but he apparently kept the title. Then, in the first half of 1971, he was finally indicted on drug charges and his time as boss came to an official end. The charges were eventually dropped, but he had already been supplanted by Natale Evola, known by his friends as "Joe Diamond." Little is known about what Sciacca did in the aftermath of his indictment and ultimate acquittal, but it's likely that he retired, or at least stepped into the background of the Family and abandoned an active role. He died in 1986.

Evola was a logical choice for Sciacca's successor. He was another old-timer who had been around to see the glory days of the small-yet-tight-knit Bonanno Family, and he had been a close associate of

Joe Bonanno since the very early days of the Mafia. He was also one of the associates that Joe brought with him to the Apalachin Meeting (the one Joe refused to admit that he had attended). He also had a good working relationship with both Vito Genovese and Carlo Gambino, two other NYC bosses. As far back as the early '30s, when the Family was just starting out, Evola was under the tutelage of Joe, driving him around and even doing security for his wedding in 1931. By Mafia standards, though, he was a bit of an odd duck. He had never taken a wife and the best evidence suggests that he continued to live with his mother for the majority of his life. Most of his contemporaries were known for having large families, but the only responsibilities Joe Diamond had were to his mother, three sisters, and the Bonanno Family, which he had been a part of since he was a young man. But this, perhaps, made him a wise choice for boss—one of the main reasons made guys tended to flip was for fear of losing income that they needed to support their families (typically, mob wives did not work). Even if Evola did go down, at least it wouldn't be a guy with a wife and kids. In any case, Evola's term as boss was another short one—in the Summer of 1973, he died of cancer.

Next in line was Philip "Rusty" Rastelli, Sciacca's one-time consigliere. Perhaps hoping that Rastelli would be a more permanent boss than the others, the Commission scheduled a sit-down in February of 1974 at Manhattan's Americana Hotel at Seventh Avenue in Midtown and officially proclaimed Rastelli as their choice for boss. Having this endorsement was a boon for the new boss, but the Family he was expected to lead was still in tatters, a seemingly helpless, glorified crew that didn't even have full Commission representation. Rastelli also represented a break in

Bonanno Family tradition. He was the first made guy that did not come from the Brooklyn faction and was made boss, which caused some resentment among the Castellammarese mafiosi, who typically hailed from Brooklyn. Rastelli did, however, also have a lot of backers besides the Commission. He had long been close allies with Dominick "Sonny Black" Napolitano, a Bonanno capo who would soon become an important figure in the Family's history and would remain one of Rastelli's biggest supporters and loyalists, even through the troubling times ahead.

Rastelli was indeed a long-serving boss, at least compared with Sciacca and Evola, but he did not have very long as a free man. For years, Rastelli had been operating a phony "trade association" for food-truck drivers and lunch wagons in New York City in which he extorted membership fees out of the drivers for "protection," and threatened those who refused to join with physical violence, destruction of property, or even death. He profited off of this scam for nearly a decade before the drivers and workers had enough and began going to the NYPD and the feds. Rusty was indicted in 1975 on extortion and racketeering charges related to the food trucks, and in April 1976 he was convicted, sentenced to a total of 14 years on charges that also included loan sharking (also referred to as "Shylocking," a reference to William Shakespeare's character Shylock, who ran a predatory money-lending business).

Even before Rastelli went away, his rivals viewed him as a weak leader despite his Commission blessing and support from various powerful elements in the admittedly weakened Family. A dangerous renegade mafioso named Carmine Galante stepped into the scene and began causing serious problems for him. Galante, a "mental dullard with the low IQ" (Scarpo, 2014), had been a long-time advisor and counselor to Joe Bonanno and had helped him orchestrate the famous Palermo deal of 1957; he also served as a key enforcer for Joe in Montreal. After several narcotics-related charges in the '50s and '60s, Galante was paroled in 1974, right around the time Rastelli was about to be sent to prison. Galante was reportedly an old friend of Rastelli, and the two got along during Joe Bonanno's era, but without the powerful influence of Don Peppino, Galante sought to strike out on his own. Under Rastelli's leadership, Galante began making cross-border narcotics deals through his extensive connections in Canada, all without the blessing or even knowledge of his superiors in New York. Worse, after Rastelli was put away, Galante made an audacious and unsanctioned attempt to seize full control of the Bonanno Family.

Carmine Galante was known to be unstable, aggressive, and incredibly and needlessly violent. He was also an exceedingly petty man—one of the first things he did upon his release from prison was to order a bomb planted at the mausoleum where Frank Costello, a former Genovese man, was buried. The blast caused significant damage to Costello's resting place—and accomplished exactly nothing. After Galante took control of the Family, he caused a tremendous amount of problems in a short period of time. Since the 1950s, many believed Galante had his eyes on seizing the drug trade for himself, and after his opportunistic power grab, he finally had the means to try to accomplish it. He began strong-arming other mafiosi who attempted to make profit from the heroin trade, and even started a small war with the Gambino Family, ordering the hits of around 10 of their guys. He made it clear that his goal was a full monopoly over the Mafia's drug rackets, and that he would tolerate absolutely zero interference.

Carmine Galante, known for his annoying habit of chain-smoking huge cigars, quickly became the most hated mobster in New York City—perhaps the country. The Gambinos obviously hated him for his greed and violence, but he was also reviled by the Genoveses as well as members of his own Family, particularly those still loyal to the imprisoned Rastelli, including capos Sonny Black Napolitano and Joe Massino. Frank Tieri, the current boss of the Genovese Family, was the first of several made guys who reached out to other Commission leaders to sanction a hit on the renegade Galante, whom he feared would bring untold destruction to New York's Mafia structure. The way he saw it, the Bonannos tearing themselves apart was one thing, but Galante posed a threat to everyone around him. Even the retired Joe Bonanno out in Arizona was contacted about the Galante situation, because the two had been so close for decades—Bonanno, likely realizing there was no way of talking sense into a psychotic man like Galante, simply acquiesced and gave his blessing for a hit. Before long, the entire Commission was in agreement—Galante had to go. In the summer of 1979, three masked gunmen walked casually up to the front dining patio of Joe and Mary's restaurant in Brooklyn, where Galante was having lunch with several made guys from his crew. The men hit Galante and two of his lunchmates with blasts from their shotguns before fleeing the scene. The police found the renegade boss lying dead next to his table, his blood draining into a nearby grate, a smoldering cigar still clenched between his teeth.

Red Vs. Black

Galante was gone and the Bonanno Family hoped this would finally usher in a new era of peace, but this was not meant to be. Rastelli's leadership faced yet another crisis, and the Family once again split into two distinct factions. One side consisted of those who still supported the imprisoned Rastelli's claim to be boss and was led by the notorious capo Dominick "Sonny Black" Napolitano. He had earned this nickname for a rather hilarious reason—unlike the majority of those of Italian descent who generally had jet black, or at least dark brown hair, Napolitano instead was stark blonde. He also turned fully gray quite early in his life and, being self-conscious of this, was known to dye his hair as black as possible to match his younger colleagues. The other faction was made up of those who wanted to abandon Rastelli completely and instead organize the Family leadership around an opposing capo, Alphonse Indelicato, commonly known as "Sonny Red." It's less clear how Indelicato earned his nickname, but he was known to almost always wear a pair of bright-red cowboy boots that he had made custom. Both Sonnys were high-ranking members of the Family, and Sonny Red was supported by other powerful caporegimes, including Dominick "Big Trin" Trinchera and Phil Giaccone, the latter of whom was an early protege of John Bonventre, one of Joe Bonanno's uncles from the Castellammarese Bonventre branch.

Sonny Black, on the other hand, ran arguably the most prestigious crew in the entire Bonanno Family, consisting of soldiers like Benjamin "Lefty" Ruggiero (also affectionately known by the nickname "Horse Cock"), Nicky Santora, John Zancocchio (who later on became the Bonanno consigliere), and the Lino brothers.

Sonny Black was also supported by strong capos like Joe Massino and Gerlando "George from Canada" Sciascia. (Joe Massino, in fact, was one of Rastelli's top supporters and many believe Sonny Black was actually the one taking orders from him. Regardless, the two were united against Sonny Red Indelicato and his mostly Sicilian faction.) The primary hangout of the Sonny Black crew was The Motion Lounge, a swanky nightclub owned by Napolitano. The club was on Graham Avenue in Williamsburg, the traditionally Castellammarese neighborhood of Brooklyn, although Napolitano traced his roots back to Naples, not Sicily (unsurprising given his last name). Sonny Black and his guys hung around Motion so often that is became their *de facto* headquarters and earned them the nickname the "Motion Lounge Crew."

Aside from just being prestigious, Sonny Black also ran easily the most profitable crew in the Family. Lefty Ruggiero was one of the top Bonanno earners and had a significant street presence and name recognition around all of New York City, not just the Brooklyn borough. Williamsburg was firmly under Sonny Black's grasp in the late '70s and '80s, and especially Graham Avenue, where the Motion Lounge was one of only two clubs that Napolitano owned, one being just across the street from the other. From their headquarters, the crew dipped their toes into every criminal racket imaginable, from small-time bookmaking to international drug smuggling to large casino operations. Just like Joe Bonanno, Napolitano also extended his influence far out of state. Being a fan of the warm weather, he branched out into Florida, where he formed a close relationship with the Trafficante Family, who operated mostly out of Tampa Bay. He owned several businesses in the Tampa area in the central-west coast of Florida, specifically in Pasco County. One of his biggest moneymakers was an underground casino-style operation, and later, he owned the King's Court, a beach-themed nightclub that he ran with the help of several of his soldiers and associates, including a gentleman by the name of Donnie Brasco. The Trafficante Family also had operations in Cuba and helped the Napolitano crew branch out to there as well (although since the Cuban Revolution of 1959, Mafia operations on the island had become severely limited and it was no longer the Caribbean cash cow it once was).

Tensions continued to rise between the Sonny Red and Black factions throughout the late '70s and early '80s. Then, in 1981, something happened that required immediate action. Sonny Black and Joe Massino learned from reliable sources that Sonny Red and his faction had been hoarding a significant stockpile of weaponry, including automatic rifles and a large amount of ammunition. It was obvious enough what their intentions were, and Sonny Black had long been suspecting it. The Red crew were gearing up and preparing for an all-out war against the rest of the Family. They were planning on taking out Napolitano, Massino, and all of the remaining supporters of the imprisoned Rusty Rastelli and seizing full control of the Bonanno Family for themselves. This obviously could not be allowed to happen, as another large-scale war would doom the already disgraced Family. With this information, Napolitano and Massino quickly contacted the bosses of the other Five Families and requested permission to organize a hit on Sonny Red, Big Trin, and Phil Giaccone, the three rebellious capos. Apparently, the Commission at large told the two captains not to take action until it was absolutely necessary so as to avoid needless bloodshed. Confidentially, though, Colombo boss Carmine Persico and Gambino boss Paul Castellano told them that defending themselves in this situation was a necessity to protect Rastelli's authority. They assured them of their support.

So, in May 1981, Sonny Red was contacted by the Black faction and asked to have a sit-down together to talk through their problems, with both sides acknowledging that the Commission did not want another war. They insisted that all three of the leading capos show up to make sure they were all on the same page and that none of them would go rogue. In reality, though, Sonny Black and Massino needed them all there so that they could be eliminated in one clean sweep. The three rebellious capos agreed to the meeting, which was to be held on May 5 at the 20/20 nightclub in Clinton Hill, Brooklyn. The Black faction ended up involving a surprising amount of made guys and associates in the scheme, and it was frankly a miracle that the Red faction never caught wind of the secret plan. They did suspect the possibility of betrayal, though, and made other members of the faction aware that if the three capos went "missing," they were to be assumed dead and should retaliate as fiercely as possible.

For support, the Black faction and Massino reached out to their contacts in the Canadian faction in Montreal. Three made guys from the Cotroni Family quickly made their way stateside to New York to help plan and execute the killings. Among them was the future notorious mob boss Vito Rizzuto, son of Nicolo Rizzuto. At the time, Rizzuto was a rising star in the Montreal mob, but the Cotronis were currently embroiled in a deadly civil war between the Calabrian and Sicilian factions, the latter of which Rizzuto helped lead. Vito had extensive connections across the world, with strong ties to the Cuntrera-Caruana Family based out of Sicily, as well as drug cartels in South America, particularly Venezuela, where he would later go to implant his Family business. He also had connections with the Hell's Angels motorcycle gang. Needless to say, he was a well-connected guy who didn't mind doing a favor for his New York colleagues if it meant it would help his own bid for power back in Montreal. With the help of their liaison Gerlando Sciascia, Rizzuto also brought his associate Emanuele Ragusa and another Montreal guy who remains unknown to this day. With this, Rizzuto would win the full support of the Bonannos, and once the civil war ended, in the mid-1980s, Vito became the number-one mob boss in Canada.

On the night of the 5th, Sonny Red and the two other capos arrived at 20/20 completely unarmed. They entered and were greeted by Massino, Sciascia, and three other mafiosi from the Rastelli loyalist faction. They said their greetings, but the three capos didn't even have a chance to sit down. Suddenly, four men who had been in hiding burst out of a couple closets nearby, armed with loaded shotguns and automatic rifles. They were Vito Rizzuto, the two other Canadians, and Salvatore Vitale, a relative of Massino's. The three capos were first physically assaulted and beaten by the gang of Rastelli's guys before finally being executed gangland style, with a barrage of gunfire. Frank Lino, who originally supported the Red faction, was also present and served as "bodyguard" for the three capos, but he clearly did a poor job. Rather than pull his weapon and retaliate, he fled as soon as the fighting started. After the capos were dead, everyone besides Massino and Vitale quickly left the scene, and Vito and his party hastily returned to Canada (this hit would later come back to haunt the Montreal don). After the hit,

Massino and Vitale quickly transported the bodies to a large, empty lot in the Queens borough, known to be a commonly used burial ground by the Gambino Family. The legendary future boss John Gotti, at the time a Gambino capo who was aware that the hit was about to go down, arranged for some associates from his crew to take care of the bodies as a personal favor to Massino and Sonny Black. The two Rastelli capos had now eliminated their biggest threat, but unbeknownst to them, an even more dire threat was still lurking in the shadows of their own crew.

Donnie Brasco

Since the 1960s, the federal and state government in New York had been looking for new and innovative ways to disrupt Mafia operations in the state and country. The easiest strategies included planting surveillance devices in known Mafia hideouts and threatening made guys and associates with harsh prison sentences unless they agreed to inform on their Mafia comrades. This latter option was particularly effective against mafiosi who dealt in the drug business. This was partly because narcotics offenses carried far stiffer penalties than they were used to, but it was also because drug-dealing mafiosi had a tendency to start sampling their own products. Especially when it came to heroin and cocaine, the guys who formed a habit generally ended up paranoid, erratic, needlessly suspicious, and, inevitably, broke. All these factors combined to make the narcotics guys very pliable. In order to save themselves and what was left of their income, they were eager to make deals with the feds who threatened them with 20 or more years in prison.

In the 1970s, this dynamic changed in an important way. Law-enforcement agencies were now also looking to get some of their own agents on the inside—they wanted firsthand accounts from within the Mafia structure. This was an audacious strategy, which would require months of extensive planning, and it carried more than a few risks to the agents who were willing to sacrifice potentially years of their life. But it also promised to be a career-making endeavor. Any federal agent would have loved to be the guy who fooled an entire Mafia Family. Longtime FBI Director J. Edgar Hoover was strictly against placing his own men inside the Mafia—he was convinced that they would end up becoming corrupt after seeing the obscene amounts of easy money they could make. But in 1972 Hoover died, and new opportunities presented themselves. In 1976, someone with the talent to pull it off stepped up to the task. His name was Joseph Dominick Pistone—he had been an FBI agent since 1969 and was already noted for his excellent undercover work.

There were a number of factors that made him well-suited to the job. He had reliable Sicilian ancestry, spoke quite good Italian (most mafiosi hadn't been fluent in Italian for decades, but it was still a noteworthy benefit for authenticity), and he had spent most of his formative years in a region of New Jersey that was known to have a significant Mafia presence. Paterson, where he grew up, was just north of Newark and Elizabeth, where the DeCavalcante Family dominated. As a result, he grew up seeing mafiosi and could easily mimic their behavior and mannerisms. Besides all this, he simply looked the part. With some nice suits, fancy shoes, and some slicking back of his hair, he could easily pass for a "connected guy." The Bureau accepted Pistone for the task, and he got to work preparing to infiltrate and ingratiate himself with the Mafia. The Family that was chosen to infiltrate was originally the Colombo Family, but in short order, Pistone and the FBI realized that the fractured and dysfunctional Bonannos would be the easier target, and their efforts shifted to Rastelli's Family.

The work creating the backstory of Donnie Brasco was in itself a months-long operation. The Bureau needed to create a convincing history, as the Mafia had a tendency of looking into the backgrounds of potential associates. They needed to hammer down exactly where Brasco was from, who his parents were, from where in the old country he traced his roots, his trade, his criminal background, and who his friends were. Regardless of the details, Brasco would have to be a relatively unknown character, because he would have no way of explaining how not a single made guy had heard of him until the operation began. So, it was decided that Donnie would be a jewel appraiser and small-time jewel thief. They even had a nickname for him—Don the Jeweler. Unfortunately for Pistone's family, the operation required more than simply tricking the New York mafiosi. The man known as "Joseph Pistone" needed to disappear. All records of his employment at the FBI were erased, all references and photographs of him were wiped. He had to abruptly cease *all* communication with his friends, and had only limited contact with his own wife and children. His wife was not even allowed to know what he was doing, simply that he was doing something for an important investigation. He could rarely return home, lest a suspicious wise guy decide to tail him one day and discover his true home and familial connections. This would've endangered not only Pistone and the mission, but his entire family. If his friends or family were to ever contact the Bureau and ask about him, they were to flatly deny that a man named Joe Pistone had ever worked for the FBI. His colleagues were instructed to lie and claim that they had never heard of anyone by that name.

Being in minimum contact with his family may have been a bearable undertaking given that the mission was meant to last a total of six months. Unfortunately, the success of the mission convinced both Pistone and the Bureau that it needed to be extended indefinitely. In total, it lasted around for six long years and, unsurprisingly, took a toll on Pistone's personal life. After months of planning, the operation began in the summer of 1976. The Bureau had been fabricating a kind of reputation for Donnie in the lead-up, and so by the time he hit the streets, some of the Colombos had already heard of Don the Jeweler. Some came to him looking to fence some gems and to get tips on jewel heists. He ended up getting close to the Colombo's Greca crew, but he formed a deeper relationship with Anthony Mirra, a capo in the Bonanno Family. Mirra was technically the one who introduced him to the Family, but Brasco ended up forming a far closer relationship with Lefty Ruggiero, one of the soldiers and prominent enforcers in Sonny Black Napolitano's crew. Donnie began working small-time operations with Lefty; he eventually was able to gain the complete trust of both the soldier and Sonny Black. However, another capo, Joe Massino, always seemed to have a deep mistrust of Donnie—despite the months of planning Brasco's history, Massino was very wary of the fact that Donnie seemed to pop up in Brooklyn out of nowhere.

Brasco continued to play his part admirably, and for his commitment to the role, he branched out and began forming Mafia connections in such far-flung areas as Wisconsin (particularly Milwaukee) and Florida. In Tampa, he was vital in Sonny Black's muscling in on the nightclub scene, and he helped run the *King's Court* bottle club there. He still maintained a presence in New York, though, and was always equipped with secret recording devices either strapped to his chest or hidden in his boots. Meanwhile, an FBI team spent sleepless nights analyzing everything that Brasco was able to listen in on. Brasco also played his part during the Red versus Black conflict, but he was expertly able to maintain the complete trust of Lefty and Sonny through the war, all without ever having to actually murder anyone, which would, of course, be grounds for ending the investigation. Undercover agents were given some leeway in what they could do to gain trust, but a federal agent committing murder was completely out of the question. This soon came to an end, though—after Indelicato and the other capos were murdered, Sonny Black had a new task for Donnie.

Bruno Indelicato, the son of the late Sonny Red, had been forewarned that his dad and his associates might get popped either at the meeting at 20/20 or shortly after. He was given clear instructions to *assume* that Sonny Black had taken him out if Sonny Red ever went missing. Knowing that his dad had no plans on going on the lam (and even if he did, he would've told Bruno), the younger Indelicato immediately realized what had happened, and he swore revenge on the Rastelli loyalist crew. Napolitano and Massino couldn't risk a new opposition crew coalescing around Bruno, so they needed to act fast. Despite Massino's distrust of the mysterious associate, Napolitano gave the contract to Donnie Brasco. This was also part of a bigger strategy by Sonny Black—he had planned on sponsoring Donnie to become a made guy immediately once Rastelli was released from prison. To do this, though, Donnie would need a lot more credibility. He would need to "make his bones"—i.e., commit a high-profile assassination on behalf of the Bonanno Family. Bruno was a perfect target. The younger Indelicato apparently knew immediately that his life was in danger, because he vanished from New York City very soon after Sonny Red's disappearance.

Most of the Family suspected that Bruno fled to Florida, where he and his father had some connections. After a sit-down at the Motion Lounge, Sonny Black officially gave Donnie the order to hunt down and murder Bruno. It would have been a massive deal. Lefty Ruggiero later confided in Donnie, "I'm really happy that he's [Sonny] having you clip Bruno, because it'll look good in the eyes of the bosses that you did some work," he said, "it's a good contract." The undercover man's only response was "yeah, I'm happy too, Left" (Pistone, 1989). But Donnie was torn between two worlds. On the one hand, he would've been assured a spot in the Family as a made guy and soldier, opening up a new world for infiltration that the FBI could only have dreamt of years ago. On the other hand, there was no way Donnie would ever assassinate someone, and even if he, as a person, was up to the task, the FBI never would have let him even get close to doing it. Further, the very fact that he had been given the contract likely meant that the Bureau would end the operation as soon as possible. The meeting with Sonny Black was recorded in its entirety, but the technology of the day was not always reliable. Soon after, Joe "Donnie Brasco" Pistone met up with federal agents in New Jersey at a little hotel they were holed up at. He told them everything that Sonny Black had told him—the info was too valuable to risk on faulty recording machines. He told them about the hits on Sonny Red's crew and the fact that Sonny Black was now the pre-eminent power in the Family, aside from the imprisoned Rusty Rastelli. Finally, he told them about his new mission to Florida to hunt down the surviving son,

Bruno. He was also given the side task of transporting some drugs (quaaludes) down to Florida to test the market—the little pills went for cheap in New York and he was hoping that Tampa Bay party kids would be willing to cough up top dollar for them.

Even before the hit order was given, Donnie had become a big name worthy of respect around New York City. Once Indelicato and his supporters were gone, Sonny Black had become arguably the most powerful man in the entire Bonanno Family. Plus, just about everyone knew that Donnie had become a close favorite of his, and according to some, he liked the associate more than most of his own soldiers. He trusted Donnie implicitly and had big plans for his future in the Family. Just about everyone treated Donnie like he was already a made man, and no one dared to run afoul with him lest they arouse the ire of the big man Sonny Black himself. The other soldiers and associates who were once under Indelicato had been falling in line and accepting the new leadership. In the new age, Donnie's loyalty would be handsomely rewarded. For the whole Family, in fact, things were looking up. Aside from Bruno, the one thorn still in their side, some semblance of control and stability was finally coming to the long-troubled Bonanno clan. As Sonny Black said in a private meeting, "this is the first time in over ten years that the Family has control over itself rather than being controlled by the Commission" (Pistone, 1989).

There was another problem, though. Word had gotten around rather quickly that the contract was out on Bruno and that Donnie Brasco was the man assigned to carry it out. Even Bruno, wherever he was, had learned that Donnie was on the job. This posed a significant risk for Brasco, and the Bureau was eager to end the mission. If the first agent they got to successfully infiltrate the Mafia at this level was to get whacked during a gang war, they could kiss all future infiltration missions goodbye. Even if the Bureau decided to continue the strategy, they would be hard-pressed to find agents willing to do the job. Pistone needed to be pulled out. Pistone vehemently disagreed, but with the knowledge that Bruno, who still had some support from his father's loyalists, would very likely be trying to whack him before he himself got killed, the agent didn't have much of a say in the matter. Plus, the news of Indelicato's death had made recent New York headlines after his body was discovered a mere few weeks after the hit. Now, every wise guy in the country knew that Sonny Black's crew had made the move. Apparently, the Gambino guys that John Gotti had bury the bodies did a very poor job—some kids had been playing around on the empty lot and one of them actually noticed a bright red cowboy boot sticking straight up out of the ground. It was Indelicato. They had buried him so shallow that you could literally kick the dirt away to reveal his body. The others, at least, were buried a bit better, and it would take a few years before they were discovered. With all this heat, the Bureau ended the "Brasco" operation a bit later in 1981, and Joe Pistone was pulled out, having exposed some of the deepest Mafia secrets in the history of law enforcement.

Pistone's case was easily the most intimate that American law enforcement had ever been able to get inside the Italian Mafia. To this day, it remains a legendary operation and is still looked to as an example of how to ingratiate oneself in the shady, seamy underworld of Mafia politics. Pistone never became a made guy, but had it not been for factors outside of his control, it would have been a matter of months before he achieved this incredible feat. Joseph

Pistone sacrificed years of his life to help bring down the Bonanno Family, and the evidence he gathered over these several years led to an immense amount of convictions and had serious ramifications for the infamous Mafia Commission Trial, which was only four short years away. For all of his hard work, dedication, and sacrifice, federal agent Pistone was given a paltry $500 bonus from the Federal Bureau of Investigation.

CHAPTER 7
The New Massino Regime

After the Donnie Brasco mission was complete, the Bureau decided to rub salt in the collective Bonanno wound. They couldn't let Sonny Black believe that Brasco had simply vanished without fulfilling the hit on Bruno. Instead, federal agents Jim Kinne, Jerry Loar, and Doug Fencl met with Napolitano and informed him that the man he took under his wing back in the late '70s was, in fact, an undercover agent. Later, it became public news that Brasco was not a real person and that the Sonny Black crew had been thoroughly infiltrated. The Bureau knew exactly what they were doing—by revealing this information to the public, Napolitano and everyone connected to Donnie were doomed. The entire Bonanno Family, in fact, was in serious trouble.

Aftermath: Brasco And The Mafia Commission Trial

Despite the rise to power of the Sonny Black crew, after the successful Indelicato hit, their poor collective judgement had allowed the federal government years of direct, intimate access to their Mafia activity. To their credit, even after being confronted with the information that Pistone was an informant, information that certainly marked them for death, the main figures still refused to turn witness to gain protection from the government. They all apparently accepted their fate rather than break *omerta*. Sonny Black was no longer the *de facto* boss; no one was a serious challenger to take his place besides Joe Massino, the next big man in charge after Rastelli. Massino, who long suspected something was "off" about Donnie, was enraged when his true identity was revealed. He and Sonny Black used to be bitter rivals before the Red versus Black conflict, but now Massino had a perfect excuse to get rid of his entire crew once and for all.

Dominick "Sonny Black" Napolitano was the first to meet retribution for the incident. On August 17, 1981, his presence was requested at a meeting ordered by Massino. Fearing that Sonny might decide to flee, Massino sent two of his guys, Frank Lino and Steve Canone, to pick him up from his home and escort him to the meeting, which was to be held at the home of Ron Filocomo, one of the Bonanno's many associates. Sonny had no illusions about what was coming—he knew he wouldn't be leaving the meeting alive. He gave away all his jewelry to one of the workers at the Motion Lounge just hours before Lino and Canone arrived. He was also known to keep pigeons on the roof of his apartment, and supposedly arranged for them to be taken care of after his death. When the pair of escorts arrived, Napolitano wordlessly got in the vehicle, likely in the front passenger seat to prevent him from attacking the two from the rear.

They arrived shortly after in Staten Island, where Ronnie Filocomo lived. The two walked the unarmed Sonny Black up to the house, where Bonanno capo Frank Coppa was waiting with the front door open. He acted friendly, but Sonny's grimacing face didn't budge. This was always how it was—when you're a made guy marked for death, you're usually surrounded by your friends, acting like they are thrilled to see you. Then when you least expect it, it's a bullet in the back of the head. Sonny wasn't fooled, but he wasn't going to resist. Coppa was a big-time Bonanno guy, very active on Wall Street and known for running "pump-and-dump" scams, where his brokers would oversell a certain stock that connected guys had shares in, which would pump up the price of the stock. Then, there would be a massive sell-off where the mafiosi involved earned massive profits, but the price of the stock would tank as a result, leaving the innocent investors with millions of dollars in losses. These lucrative schemes, which Coppa pioneered, earned him "made man" status in 1977 by none other than the mentally ill renegade boss Carmine Galante. Coppa would also end up betraying the Family decades later, though, when he turned state witness to save himself from prison in the early 2000s.

Sonny Black entered the home after the standard greetings were exchanged between Coppa and the other three, but there was clearly no meeting being held. Coppa motioned Sonny toward the door to the basement, where he said that the real meeting would take place. If Sonny Black weren't already aware of his fate, this definitely would have made him suspicious. Regardless, Sonny dutifully opened the door and was the first to descend the staircase toward the armed gunmen awaiting him below. Just then, Sonny felt the full force of his fellow mobsters' weight behind him as they brutally shoved him down the flight of stairs. He tumbled all the way to the bottom, where Filocomo and Bob Lino already had their pistols drawn, pointed at the injured Naplitano. Even in death, though, Napolitano was graceful. Just before the pair unloaded their clips into the disgraced captain, he uttered his last words: "make it a good one" (Raab, 2005). After he was dead, Napolitano's hands were severed and disposed of to prevent police from identifying his body from his fingerprints.

Lefty Ruggiero, one of Sonny Black's soldiers and one of Donnie's closest friends while he was undercover, was next. After the news of Donnie's identity broke, Lefty allegedly refused to believe it. He and Donnie were too close, and he believed that it was in fact an FBI ploy designed to sow discontent within the Family. Whether or not Lefty was simply in denial, we can't say for sure, but it didn't change Joe Massino's mind. Lefty, too, was marked for death. Luckily, fate intervened. While he was on his way to the meeting where he was to be murdered, on August 29, 1981, just weeks after Napolitano's death, Lefty was intercepted by FBI agents. Even while he was in jail awaiting trial for racketeering, he refused to believe Donnie was an informant. He maintained this all the way until Joe Pistone officially testified against him in court. The following November, Ruggiero was sentenced to 15 years, along with fellow Bonanno soldiers Nicky Santora and Tony Rabito. Almost exactly 12 years later, Lefty died from cancer.

Tony Mirra, the guy who first introduced Donnie to Lefty and the Sonny Black crew, was the last of the three to be dealt with. He proved a bit more cowardly than the other two—immediately after the infiltration was revealed, Mirra went into hiding. It was months before the Family discovered his whereabouts. Massino ended up giving the contract to Joe D'Amico, one of Mirra's cousins, because he was the only one that Mirra would likely be willing to meet with. Around mid-February 1982, D'Amico met up with Mirra in a New York City parking garage. D'Amico hopped into the car that Mirra was driving and as they prepared to leave together, D'Amico shot

Mirra in the head at close range. D'Amico then hopped back out and got in a hidden getaway car where Mirra's uncle Alfred "Al Walker" Embarrato and his other cousin Richie "Shellackhead" Cantarella were waiting. They sped off, the score with Donnie's sponsors having finally been settled.

The Bonanno Family, once again, was in shambles. The Sonny Black crew was without a leader and their reputation was permanently tarnished. Even though Rastelli was in prison during the fiasco, he was still ultimately responsible as he had vouched for Sonny Black, who, in turn, vouched for a federal undercover agent (not to mention very nearly inducted him into their Family). Even with Napolitano, Ruggiero, and Mirra gone, it did little to appease the rest of the Five Families. As a final punishment for the Donnie Brasco incident, the Mafia Commission officially removed Rastelli and the entire Bonanno Family from the Commission. They weren't just without a seat at the table; they were now severed from the entire Commission structure. This was a tragedy on paper, but there were benefits to this, as well, as we will soon see. Joe Massino was now the *heir apparent* to the old man Rusty Rastelli.

Rastelli was finally released from prison in April 1983. He was welcomed back to a disgraced and defeated Family, but he wouldn't be among them for very long—he would be on his way back to prison in less than a year. Almost immediately after his release, Rastelli and Massino organized a hit on another Bonanno capo, Cesare "Tall Guy" Bonventre of the notorious Bonventre clan that traced its roots back to the same Sicilian town as the Bonannos and Magaddinos. This was likely an attempt to "tighten up" the Family and consolidate Rastelli's control over it. Bonventre was the head of the Bonannos' Zips faction and had steadily been growing his power base while the rest of the Family was consumed with infighting and civil wars. ("Zip" is a slang term for mafiosi who were born in Sicily or the Italian mainland and who later migrated to America—as opposed to American-born mafiosi.) Bonventre, with his loyal and brutal crew of Italians, posed a threat to Rastelli, and by extension, his heir Massino. Plus, Bonventre was already in pretty serious legal trouble for his involvement in the Sicilian heroin smuggling racket. Rather than risk him trying to seize power, or flip and become a witness to avoid prison, he was marked for death. Sal Vitale and Louis Attanasio were given the job. They picked up the Sicilian and drove him to a phony sit-down in New Jersey, and as they parked, Attanasio unloaded to bullets into the back of his head. Bonventre either had an incredibly thick skull, or he was just one tough bastard—with two bullets lodged in his head, he still had the strength to try to kill his two assassins. After very nearly crashing the car into the building, Vitale and Attanasio finally overpowered him and killed him as he tried to crawl away. Shortly after he died and his body was disposed of, Bonventre was indicted on the drug charges. Unbeknownst to law enforcement, he was already dead.

Also in 1984, boss Philip Rastelli was arrested once again, this time for violating the terms of his parole. He was prohibited from associating with known criminals while on parole, which was a common condition for early release. Rastelli apparently wasn't careful enough, though, as officers had witnessed him at meetings with other members of his Family. In 1985, his legal troubles got much worse. That year, Rastelli, as well as every other head of the NYC Five Families, was indicted on federal charges in the most devastating legal case against the Mafia in the history of organized crime. It was the Mafia Commission Trial, and it struck at the very heart of the American Mafia leadership. Even though the Bonannos' Donnie Brasco incident caused intense embarrassment and legal trouble for the Mafia, it was ultimately the Lucchese Family that brought the most significant heat down on Italian-American organized crime.

Within the first few years of the '80s, Lucchese boss Anthony "Tony Ducks" Corallo had established a virtual monopoly over the waste-disposal business on Long Island. Small business owners were threatened with violence unless they paid tribute to the Lucchese Family in exchange for "protection" over their garbage routes. The majority of them caved to the mob's aggressive extortion tactics, but one stood out. His name was Rob Kubecka, and he owned a local hauling business. He also flat-out refused to be taken advantage of. As a result, he was frequently harassed and threatened, and Lucchese associates routinely tried to disrupt his business (Rob had actually inherited the business from his father, who also had consistently denied the Lucchese attempts to muscle in on his business). Gangsters damaged his trucks, slashing tires and smashing windows, starting fires, and even threatening his customers with violence if they used Kubecka's routes.

Eventually, the small-business owner had enough—he went to the FBI. He agreed to set up a meeting with Lucchese Family members, and he also agreed to wear a hidden listening device to record the entire conversation. The meeting was held sometime in 1982, and the FBI successfully picked up Lucchese guys threatening and extorting him. This was enough evidence to convince a Long Island judge to allow the Bureau to set up more wiretaps, including in the personal vehicle and home of Sal Avellino, one of Corallo's captains. The bugs in his car were most successful, and the FBI picked up crystal-clear audio of Corallo, Avellino, and other made guys directly referencing the highly secretive Mafia Commission. They discussed its leadership structure, how and why it functioned, its democratic nature, Mafia membership practices, and much more. Over the course of the investigation, the men also directly implicated each and every one of the other Five Family bosses. The recordings were a veritable gold mine.

These recordings ultimately led to the 1985 indictments of Lucchese boss Anthony Corallo, Gambino boss Paul Castellano, Genovese boss Anthony "Fat Tony" Salerno, and of course, Bonanno boss Rusty Rastelli. Later on, Colombo boss Carmine Persico was indicted as well. The heads of every major New York City Family were now at risk of being put in prison for the rest of their lives, as were top-ranking subordinates from each Family. For the Bonannos, Rastelli was obviously the prime target, but Stefano Canone (allegedly the Family consigliere at the time) and Anthony "Bruno" Indelicato (son of slain capo Sonny Red Indelicato) were also indicted. This massive court case came to be known as the Mafia Commission Trial of 1985, and it threatened to dismantle the entire New York City criminal underworld. In the end, the Luccheses and Colombos were hit the hardest. The Lucchese Family lost their boss, underboss, and their consigliere, who each received 100 years in prison, and between them, they were fined $750,000. Their entire leadership structure was put in prison. The other Families all had at least their bosses convicted, except the Gambinos. Paul Castellano was assassinated before a verdict was handed down, but he very likely would have been convicted too. Rastelli actually got off quite easy by a twist of fate.

Rastelli was still put in prison, but not directly as a result of the Commission Trial. In May 1984, in a secret Staten Island meeting, four Family bosses met to discuss the details of a lucrative construction racket scheme they had all taken part of. Because of Donnie Brasco, which led to the utter distrust of the Bonanno Family and their Commission status, Rastelli was not invited to take part in the scheme, nor were any Bonanno Family guys or representatives. This happened to be the case that led to the most severe convictions for the bosses. Because Rastelli was not directly involved, and because his Family was now a completely separate entity from the Commission, the charges against him in this case were ultimately dropped. The four other Families had their chains of command fractured, but the Bonannos "dodged a big bullet and continued to operate with much of its leadership intact," and they were later able to "consolidate and recover from the disaster of L'Affaire Brasco" (Destefano, 2008). Still, Rastelli didn't have as much luck as the rest of the Bonannos. He was still under investigation and indictment in a parallel trial that ended with his conviction 1986. He received 12 years behind bars on 24 separate counts of racketeering charges.

Between 1985 and 1987, there was another legal problem for the Bonannos and the other Families, particularly their Sicilian factions that operated most of the international drug trade from Europe into Canada into the US. It came to be known as the "Pizza Connection Trial" and it saw more than a dozen convictions of important American and Sicilian mobsters. The state alleged that organized criminals were using various pizza joints around New York City as fronts to house and distribute narcotics brought in from out of the country. It once again threatened the biggest moneymaking operation for a huge number of mafiosi. The Bonanno Family was especially vulnerable—most of the Canadian connections in the drug trafficking operation were theirs, and it was Joe that was behind the 1957 Palermo meeting that organized much of the details. Gaetano Badalamenti, one of the Sicilian bosses that was present for the Palermo meeting, was also one of those indicted in the Pizza Connection Trial, and he could have had much to say about that Family's involvement. In 1987 the verdicts were handed down and Gaetano, among others, was sent to prison. It wasn't the Sicilian don that did the most damage, though—FBI agent Joseph "Donnie Brasco" Pistone also took the stand as a witness to testify against the Family that he had infiltrated them years ago. Pistone directly implicated the Bonannos in the Sicilian connection and testified that the former crew of Dominick "Sonny Black" Napolitano had been the main point of contact between the Bonannos and Salvatore Catalano, one of the other main Sicilian mobsters indicted in the Pizza Connection.

Overall, the Bonannos still got off easy compared with their fellow NYC Families. Bruno Indelicato was eventually indicted, as well, which may have been a benefit to the Family, considering his vendetta against Rastelli and his underlings for the death of his father. Indelicato, however, was convicted separately on murder charges for his part in the assassination of the rogue drug kingpin boss Carmine Galante, and he received less than half the time of the Lucchese, Gambino, Genovese, and Colombo bosses, almost all of whom died in federal custody. The Commission Trial closed another brutal and unfortunate chapter in the history of the American Mafia, and in a surprising change of fortune, the Bonannos were the only ones that still looked like a real, functioning Family in its aftermath. Perhaps things would now start looking up for the Family that had been struggling for decades to regain its former glory. But with Rastelli once again forced to lead the Family from behind bars, their power would need to coalesce around a new figure. That figure would be the prominent Bonanno capo Joseph Charles Massino.

The Massino Family?

In total, Rusty Rastelli spent barely three years of his time as Bonanno boss outside of prison. Because of his chronic absence, he served as an almost mythical figure in the Family, with most of the younger mafiosi having never even met the man. Meanwhile, the day-to-day operations were being run by various capos as they struggled for dominance (i.e., Sonny Red, Black, and Joe Massino). By the time Rastelli went back to jail for the last time, in the late '80s, only one of his proteges was still around—Massino. Both Sonnys were dead, and no one else posed a real challenge. Rastelli continued to serve as the official head of the Bonannos for the rest of the '80s, while Massino, who was instilled with the values of loyalty, kept the Family in line in his stead. Rastelli's health continued to deteriorate with each passing year behind bars until he was released from prison in 1991 on compassionate leave when the government realized he didn't have much time left. They were right—just 20 days after he became a free man, he died at age 73 from advanced cancer of the liver. The Bonannos needed a new leader, ideally one who could stay out of prison for more than a few years.

Unfortunately, their next choice for boss was already imprisoned. In 1987, Massino, who was functioning as Bonanno underboss (and acting boss) for Rastelli, was sent to join Rusty in prison. He was on trial for murder and racketeering (specifically truck hijacking), and the mob informant Joe Pistone, a.k.a. Donnie Brasco, testified against him. He was ultimately acquitted for the homicides but convicted for the hijackings. It was, surprisingly, Massino's first prison bid, and he got 10 years for it. The Bonannos were now two layers deep in acting bosses, with both Rastelli and Massino off the streets. In their absence, the Family was run by a combination of capo Salvatore Vitale, who was Massino's brother-in-law, and the elderly consigliere Tony Spero. After Rastelli died, in 1991, Sal Vitale called a meeting of all the other Family capos to determine what their new course of action would be—i.e., who their next official boss would be. In reality, though, it was a foregone conclusion. Even in prison, no one had the power and influence that Massino did, and Vitale, the next most powerful captain, was loyal to his sister's husband. Plus, Massino had secretly been waiting patiently for Rastelli's death, and he had told Vitale that once Rusty was out of the picture, he needed to make sure the other capos got in line behind Massino's leadership.

Massino was successful. At Vitale's meeting, the other capos agreed that Massino, as Rastelli's heir apparent, was the only logical choice for the next boss, despite still serving a jail sentence. Vitale would continue to function as acting boss and the liaison between Massino and the rest of the Family. The Bonannos were still in bad standing with the Mafia Commission, so there was no need to bother waiting for the Commission to approve Massino. Besides, the other four

NYC Families were still reeling from the Commission Trial, so they were in no position to exert much pressure on the Bonannos.

In 1991, Massino was not yet 50 years old. This meant that he could potentially have a long reign as Bonanno boss, as long as he could guide his Family through these difficult years and steer them away from the crippling legal issues and general sloppiness that had been plaguing them for years. To have any hope of accomplishing this, however, he needed to institute sweeping reforms and eliminate the tendencies that always seemed to get made guys and associates in trouble. One of the biggest changes he put in place was a complete ban on the traditional Mafia hangout areas, which included a demand for his top guys to shut down or stop using their various social clubs. It clearly wasn't good to have well-known places where the feds knew they could always find wise guys. The idea was that having mafiosi routinely congregating in supposedly "safe spaces" made them lower their guard. Plus, they would be the most obvious locations for law enforcement to target with hidden recorders, wiretaps, and bugs. The era of infamous mob haunts like Sonny Black's Motion Lounge needed to become a thing of the past. Massino also insisted that his guys sever almost all Bonnano business ties to the other Families and criminal organizations in an effort to close ranks. Massino wanted to try as much as possible to keep their operations in-house to prevent guys from other Families from exposing Bonanno made men if they got themselves pinched.

Near the end of 1992, Massino was released from prison early on conditions of supervised release. The restrictions he was given were similar to Rastelli's when he got out back in the early '80s: He could not under any circumstances be seen associating with known mobsters or other criminals, much less be caught actually participating in crimes. He was determined to avoid the same mistakes his predecessor made. Even though he was a free man, he could still have been in prison for all his Family knew. Hardly anyone from the Family, even high-ranking guys, was allowed to see or talk to him. The one exception was Sal Vitale, Bonanno underboss, who continued to serve as Massino's go-between even while he was out on supervised release. Anything Massino needed to hear was told to him by Vitale, and anything Massino needed to tell anyone else was entrusted to Vitale and no one else. This worked for two reasons: First, Vitale had a relatively clean record and hadn't been convicted for any Mafia-related crimes during his long career. The FBI still suspected him, of course, but meeting with someone who couldn't be proven to be a mafioso wouldn't be enough to violate the terms of his conditional release. And second, Vitale and Massino were related through marriage, and so they had plausible deniability if any cop or fed went around asking why the two were meeting at one or the others' houses—especially if their wives were present. They could simply claim they were attending a family function, not a clandestine mob meeting. Things continued like this for some time, and Massino was well-insulated from the nitty-gritty of the Bonanno Family business, all the while giving orders from behind the curtain.

Even with Vitale in place as his liaison, Massino needed to make sure he wasn't implicated in case any of his guys got secretly recorded on FBI tapes like the Lucchese captain who had name-dropped his boss. To that end, Massino demanded that none of his men so much as utter his name when discussing family business. Instead, they were told to point to or touch their ears when referring to him, a tactic that he borrowed from the notoriously paranoid (and likely mentally ill) boss of the Genovese Family, Vincent Gigante. It was about the only thing that Massino admired about the erratic and unstable Genovese boss, as he had previously supported the rebel faction led by Sonny Red against Rastelli, Massino's mentor. Massino had also learned from the mistakes of his formerly very close ally, the legendary John Gotti. Since Gotti became boss of the Gambino Family (and even before), he had been making a very big name for himself, but not in a good way. He had a lust for the spotlight and, in no time at all, he had become the most recognizable and notorious crime figure in the country. This had contributed to his 1992 conviction that would see him behind bars for the rest of his life. This was a fate that Massino desperately wanted to avoid, and he criticized his friend for gaining such name recognition—it made him a huge target for the FBI. Massino, on the other hand, didn't want anyone to know who he was, and he avoided the spotlight like the plague.

Under these conditions, Joe Massino ran his new regime. There was another issue that was still bothering him, however—the Family's namesake. Massino had a serious grudge against the former boss Joe Bonanno, and not just because of his audacious power-grab that resulted in the once-great Bonanno Family being exiled as pariahs from the Mafia world. The fact that Don Peppino had actually voluntarily authored a tell-all book that spilled the secrets of not only his Family but the entire Mafia structure still enraged Massino, who considered himself an old-school gangster that lived and breathed the traditional laws of the Mafia. He didn't believe that Bonanno deserved to still have his name attached to the organization that he had disgraced, so Massino decided to give the order that all his men stop referring to themselves as the Bonanno Family. From now on, they were a part of the Massino Family, something he considered to be an entirely separate entity from the dead-and-gone Bonanno Family. Of course, he didn't want this catching on outside the Mafia, because it would have obvious implications for his personal role, and the FBI would certainly be interested in why, exactly, the man who was supposed to be keeping his nose clean suddenly had his name attached to a notorious criminal organization. The Bonanno name was dead inside the Family while he was boss, but the media, law enforcement, and the public at large continued to refer them using the old Castellammarese boss's last name. To this day, very few people refer to them as anything but the Bonanno Family.

The Donnie Brasco incident, even in the early '90s, was still looming large in the minds of Massino and the Bonanno Family leadership. FBI agent Joseph Pistone had shown that he was more than willing to testify against those he once considered friends, and his actions directly led to the death of Massino's biggest ally in the Red versus Black conflict, as well as those of some of the Bonannos' key enforcers on the street. In reality, anyone could have fallen for the scheme; it was just unlucky that it happened to take place in the crew of Dominick Napolitano and Lefty Ruggiero. Considering how successful the Brasco operation had been for the FBI, Massino knew it was only a matter of time before the Bureau made more, even bolder attempts to infiltrate the Mafia, and so more precautions needed to be taken. Even though the Commission was no longer overseeing Bonanno's affairs, including membership, Massino took it upon himself to close ranks and strictly limit the number of new inductees into the Family and his crew. Pistone had been an associate of the Bonannos for less than five years before Napolitano put him up for consideration to be made, and it likely would have happened even earlier had Rusty Rastelli not been in prison at the time. From now on, all prospective associates would need to have been known personally by a made man *for nearly a decade* before they could even be considered for admission into the Family. On top of that, the made man that sponsored them needed to vouch for them and their character personally. Everyone knew what happened to Sonny Black and Tony Mirra, so made guys needed to be absolutely sure that the guy they were vouching for was trustworthy, because their life depended on it. Unfortunately, these strict standards were not always adhered to, and the Family would suffer for it in the years to come.

After taking the reins and imposing new restrictions on membership, Massino also started encouraging made guys in the Family to start involving their sons and other male relatives in the Mafia life. The logic here was that capos and soldiers would be far less willing to turn state witness if their testimonies had the potential of endangering their own family members. It was, of course, very optimistic to assume that mobsters would hesitate to rat out their own relatives, because 70 years of Mafia history had already proven that, when put to the test, wise guys were more than willing to betray or even kill their uncles, cousins, brothers, and nephews to save themselves. Regardless, it was also an attempt to bring the Family back to their roots, to the earliest days of the Bonannos when the Family was made up almost entirely of relatives from just a handful of Castellammare del Golfo's premiere mob families, like the Bonannos and Bonventres.

Massino did not completely isolate the Family, though. He worked hard to restrengthen ties to the powerful Montreal don Vito Rizzuto, whose Family was once considered just a faction of the Bonannos but had since become independent to a degree due to the Mafia's legal issues and leadership struggles in the US. Later in the decade though, Massino apparently gave the order to have Gerlando "George from Canada" Sciascia, the long-time link between the Bonannos and their Canadian factions, killed. In 1999 he told underboss Sal Vitale that he wanted him dead, and to make sure that the scene looked like a narcotics deal gone awry. The order was delegated down the chain and it ended up being John Joseph Spirito and Patrick DeFilippo who carried out the hit. The three mobsters were driving together to a phony drug meeting, and Sciascia was shot dead in the car. The two killers then dumped his body out in public on the street to make it look like he was killed in a drive-by shooting. According to Vitale, Massino desperately needed everyone to believe that the Bonanno Family had nothing to do with Sciascia's death, because he was generally well-liked and he didn't want his guys to know he ordered a death of one of their own; he did not want to ruin his relationship with the Rizzutos. Apparently, the boss put on some theatrics to convince his guys. He feigned outrage about the killing to his capos and soldiers, and demanded that all his capos reach out to their contacts to try to discover Gerlando's killer. Unfortunately for him, very few seemed to believe his act, including Vito Rizzuto.

The Sciascia murder would come back to haunt Massino later, but for now, he had taken plenty of steps to insulate himself from the law's efforts to imprison him, and he had put measures in place to try to dissuade his own guys from turning on him, but there was still one other incentive that drove guys to flip and turn witness: money. Typically, when a mobster was thrown in prison, they lost the ability to generate income for themselves, which also meant that their wife and kids had no money coming in. These guys had to rely on the goodwill of their fellow mobsters to provide for their family while they were away, and this goodwill was not always readily available in the cutthroat and greedy game of mob life. If a guy was going away for 20 years and had no familial connections on the outside, why bother coughing up cash for his family? Their wives and kids couldn't do anything about it, and it would be decades before they'd be a free man, anyway. Alternatively, the FBI would often allow mafiosi to continue earning money as long as they supplied them with dirt on their friends. So, if a guy got pinched, they could either stick to their "code of honor" and risk losing everything, or they could keep making money while also avoiding prison—it was usually an easy decision.

To try to prevent this, Massino instituted a kind of Mafia welfare program, where every Bonanno capo and soldier would pay a special fee each month that would be placed in a legal aid fund. Any Bonanno guys that got picked up for crimes related to Family business would have their legal fees and expenses paid for out of this fund, rather than having to pay out of pocket or dig into their family's savings. After all, one of the main reasons that guys flipped was because investigators and prosecutors would intentionally drag out investigations and court cases until they inevitably bankrupted the guy they were investigating, leaving them with no more options. With this special fund, Massino hoped to eliminate one more incentive for his men to turn into rats. The program wasn't without its problems, though—several made guys took issue with the fact that they had yet another fee on top of their monthly tribute that they had to kick up to the boss, and more than one of them believed that Massino may have been skimming off the top and only set up the fund to enrich himself with the payments.

Some distrust toward Massino was mounting in the mid-'90s. A lot of it was driven by his own distrust of others. Starting in around 1995, Massino's relationship with Sal Vitale seemed to inexplicably sour. The boss took more and more responsibilities away from his underboss, and Vitale claimed that he felt he had become little more than a figurehead. The underboss of any Family often serves as a middleman between the boss and the capos, but Massino had supposedly instructed all Bonanno capos to stop talking to Vitale. He had very little authority over the Family's lower-ranking members and he was seldom used by Massino for anything other than planning hits, as he would later do with the Sciascia murder. Vitale was still allowed to earn, but he grew more and more concerned that he would be totally cut off. He also feared for his loved ones: "the loss of status had gnawed at Vitale and he felt vulnerable, believing his wife and children would be left in the street if anything ever happened" (DeStefano, 2008). The Bonannos were beginning to truly eclipse their fellow Five Families, but perhaps Massino's level of power was getting the better of him.

The new rules and reforms set in place by Massino's new, supposedly strict, regime were largely successful. The Bonannos looked like a much different Family than the one that had been eating itself alive for years with constant infighting and bosses that were either in and out of jail, or who barely survived long enough to make any impact at all. They also began, once again, to take the shape of a Family that was capable of commanding a leading role in New York's underworld. In fewer than six years as boss, Massino had become the number-one crime lord still walking free in the state of New York—possibly the entire country. The other Five Families were still struggling, even the powerful and brutally vicious Genoveses. In the time since Massino took over for the late Rusty Rastelli, the other Families had also gone through another round of mass convictions. Gambino boss John Gotti was put away for life without the possibility of parole in 1992, largely thanks to the now-infamous Mafia rat "Sammy the Bull" Gravano. Lucchese boss Vittorio Amuso and Colombo acting boss Victor "Little Vic" Orena were also slapped with life in prison (Orena got a whopping three life sentences) in 1992. Vincent "Chin" Gigante, the Genovese boss whose erratic behavior earned him the nickname "The Oddfather," was sent to prison at the end of 1997, and received 12 years plus a 1.25 million fine. Through all this, Massino was still standing tall, at least for the next few years. New York City, at long last, once again belonged to the Bonanno Family.

CHAPTER 8
Massino, Mancuso, And The Mafia In The 2020s

By the late 1990s, the FBI was becoming more and more frustrated at the rejuvenation of the Bonanno Family and their inability to nail Joe Massino on anything concrete. The new millennium presented fresh opportunities to break down the Family though; it would only be a matter of years before Massino's new regime would start to fracture. In the early 2000s, underboss Sal Vitale, who had fallen out of favor with Massino, was being investigated for crimes related to mob extortion. He ended up pleading guilty in 2001, and the next year, he pled guilty to additional charges for his loansharking racket. Vitale was put under home confinement and monitoring rather than being sent to prison right away, which led Massino to believe that his underboss had actually cut a deal with the FBI. Anyone else in the Family would have received a much harsher sentence, Massino thought. Vitale was swiftly demoted, and the man tapped to take his spot was Richard Cantarella, one of the men responsible for the hit on Tony Mirra years earlier as part of the retribution for the Donnie Brasco infiltration. It was obviously a step up for "Shellackhead" Cantarella, but he did not have much to celebrate, as he would soon discover. As an attempt to wind their way up to Massino, the FBI had begun investigating Cantarella and looking for ways to flip him, as well as other high-ranking Bonanno guys.

Sometime in the year 2000, the FBI found a way in—through one of their business associates, a man named Barry Weinberg, who owned several paid parking lots around the city. Weinberg had partnered with several higher-ups in the Bonanno Family, including Massino himself, as well as Sal Vitale and Cantarella. So, Weinberg was looped into the investigation and the team assigned to the Bonannos soon discovered that the parking-lot kingpin had millions of dollars worth of income in unpaid taxes to the IRS dating back to at least the late '80s. This was the hook that they needed. In early 2001, the team of agents picked up Weinberg, presenting him with what they had on him. They dangled the prospect of spending years in prison in his face but offered him a way out. Perhaps the FBI and the IRS could look past his phony tax statements if he were to do a little undercover work against his business partners. Apparently, Weinberg folded quite easily. He even agreed to wear a wire and set up meetings with Cantarella and his crew to record whatever illicit subjects came up in conversation. While the recording devices were live, they picked up Cantarella clearly incriminating both himself and the Bonanno boss, speaking openly about their extortion tactics as well as their loansharking and gambling rackets. Cantarella even blabbed about kidnappings the Family was involved in, as well as a high-profile murder case of *New York Post* employee Robert Perrino dating back to the early '90s.

Around 1992, state law-enforcement agencies began investigating the *Post* because evidence was mounting that Bonanno Family mobsters had undue influence in the running of the paper, which included a number of so-called "no show" jobs, paid positions at a company held by individuals who collected a handsome salary while their job description did not require their presence at the company. Essentially, they were useless positions with no responsibilities designed to siphon income into the accounts of mobsters. Robert Perrino was one of the men investigated, as he was known to be running scams at the paper under the protection of Bonanno guys. The Bonanno leadership caught wind of the state's investigation and believed that Perrino would likely be the easiest target involved to flip—he needed to be taken care of. Under the direction of Massino, Vitale, and consigliere Tony Spero, the *New York Post* superintendent was assassinated. His disappearance was long assumed to be the work of a Bonanno guy, and about a decade later, federal authorities got all the evidence they needed.

In late 2002, about 20 soldiers and associates of the powerful Bonanno Family were arrested and hit with RICO lawsuits. The feared RICO suits were the results of the 1970 RICO (Racketeer Influenced and Corrupt Organizations) Act, and they wreaked havoc on the Mafia from the late '70s onward. This allowed for two important provisions: First, they allowed prosecutors to draw direct links between criminals within an organization. If an individual was charged with a crime—loansharking, for example—and that crime was found to have been committed in the service of a broader criminal syndicate, prosecutors could attempt to draw links all the way up to the organization's leader, under whose direction that crime would be assumed to have been carried out. Second, it allowed for the seizure of an accused individual's assets that may be reasonably expected to have been obtained through criminal activity. This was serious These were very expensive cases to fight, and very often mobsters would go broke well before their case was settled. Aside from this, they also typically carried much more severe penalties upon conviction. RICO suits had the potential to decimate entire crews and even Families.

In the mass indictments of 2002, Richie Cantarella was not spared. One of their capos, Frank Coppa, was also indicted. Months earlier, Coppa had already been sent to prison on a seven-year bid for his leadership role in the Bonanno pump-and-dump investment fraud racket, whereby stockbrokers were extorted to inflate the value of a company in which the Bonannos held large amounts of shares. So, he was already serving some time before the Weinberg case fell into his lap. Born in 1941, Coppa wasn't terribly old when he received the first sentence and he apparently had a strong enough constitution to refuse to inform on his friends while serving it. But with RICO charges of extortion brought on by Weinberg's recordings—and there were plenty with Coppa's voice—he was facing the prospect of never seeing the light of day as a free man again. This would have been a tough pill for anyone to swallow, and it was certainly too much for Coppa. It did not take a whole lot of convincing to get him to cooperate against the Family: he "didn't want to die in prison away from his grandchildren and decided to make a deal" (DeStefano, 2008). Even Massino's supposed prison fund, which he was likely pilfering from anyway, could not prevent life sentences.

So it was that captain Frank Coppa became the first made guy in the Bonanno Family to agree to inform on the Family. All the steps Massino had taken and all the precautions he put in place to prevent this type of thing were for naught. This proved to be a problem for a ton of guys, because Coppa had gotten around and had plenty of dirt on Bonanno guys through his various criminal activities. Still, it was only the first domino to fall in a long line of guys soon to turn government witness. During interviews with Coppa, the capo implicated Richie Cantarella in the as-yet-unsolved murders of both Tony Mirra and the more recent Robert Perrino. The rest of the Family soon learned about Coppa's treachery—Cantarella in particular feared that he now had no realistic chance of getting away with the two homicides plus the rest of his racketeering charges. He was now in much the same position as Coppa—he had no sunny route out of his problem that didn't involve turning against his friends and associates. Canterella accepted the deal the prosecutors gave him in late 2002, and he joined Coppa in spilling whatever he knew about the Bonanno Family's activity to the feds and state authorities.

Sal Vitale was also implicated by both Coppa and Cantarella. Aside from his crimes and racketeering, they also told the FBI about his deteriorated relationship with the boss Massino, even telling them that the don had gone back and forth about having Vitale killed, eventually putting a contract on his head. So, when Vitale was arrested and charged in early 2003, along with Lino and even Joe Massino himself, they prosecutors had more than enough ammunition to try to flip the underboss as well. When Vitale learned that not only were Coppa and Cantarella implicating him in anything and everything, but that Massino had crossed the line from simply shelving his brother-in-law to actually having him whacked, his previous steadfast loyalty went out the window. Vitale was the next major figure to flip within just a few months. Vitale, given his position, knew a lot about the Bonanno business, and news of him being an informant sent panic throughout the entire Family. Guys started flipping left and right after Vitale started talking, and the more who flipped, the more it eroded everyone's sense of loyalty—"no one wanted to be the sad gangster left to face the full wrath of the courts without a cooperation agreement and with the fingers of their former colleagues-in-arms...all pointing at them in court" (Lamothe & Humphreys, 2008).

Frank Lino soon followed behind Vitale, likely due to the fact that he and the underboss had been involved in the planning of numerous homicides over the years, and there was no reason he could think of that Vitale would spare Lino from the consequences. Many powerful capos and soldiers were now working with the prosecution in exchange for greatly reduced sentences, and most were destined for witness protection upon their release. James Tartaglione, another Bonanno capo, willingly decided to flip in the midst of all the chaos, and he wasn't even under indictment yet. The situation was looking incredibly grim for boss Joe Massino, who had witnessed the integrity of his entire Family crumble before his eyes. When he eventually took the stand, he faced "testimony from a parade of turncoat mobsters" (*The Herald Times*, 2004). He was looking at a severe sentence that would likely see him die in prison from 11 RICO charges ranging from extortion, racketeering, arson, and murder, including that of Mirra and Sonny Black Napolitano, both of whom had disappeared in the '80s following the Brasco investigation. There was another murder they were investigating him for though: Gerlando "George from Canada" Sciascia. The trial for this was set to take place after the other RICO suits, but if found guilty, Massino would be facing a possible sentence of death, a punishment that was recommended for consideration by the prosecutors.

On July 30, 2004, Massino was read a guilty verdict for the initial RICO charges, which entailed life in prison on top of a fine of about $10 million. Finally, the Bonanno boss was brought down, the last of the NYC Five Family leaders to be sent to prison. After he was convicted with ease in the first trial, it appeared very likely that he was headed for another guilty verdict for the Sciascia hit. So many of his former friends were against him, guys whose loyalty he had never before questioned. Each of them was eager to point to Massino as the one guy who really ran things, the one guy who was *truly* guilty. It's safe to say that Massino likely lost all of his faith in the honor of the Mafia between 2001 and 2004. The code of *omerta* was no more, just a bygone custom of more respectful times. Everyone else around him was selling out to save themselves—why should he be the lone mafioso martyr to take all of the punishment on the chin? What incentive did he have now to keep his mouth shut? His honor wouldn't mean much if the state decided to take his life. With that, Massino ironically, yet unsurprisingly, became the first boss of one of the Five Families to fully and willingly cooperate with the state. Apparently, he sought out a deal on his own.

Massino agreed to wear a recording device when his Mafia associates came to him to discuss business while he was in prison, and he would later appear in court as witnesses against other mobsters under investigation. Between Vitale and Massino, they were responsible for putting dozens and dozens of made guys behind bars. The Bonanno Family, once considered the organization with the strictest sense of discipline and loyalty, was now the number-one source of Mafia rats. Massino was still facing life in prison, but at least he wasn't going to be put to death in this new deal, and his family would be taken care of while he wasted away without access to the riches that he spent his life chasing. Years later, in 2013, after appearing in court to testify against his former colleagues like Vincent Basciano, who was on trial for murder, and Tony Romanello, a captain in the Genovese Family, Massino was granted supervised release. Basciano had been serving as acting boss of the Family before Massino flipped and while a huge chunk of the rest of the Family were under mass indictments. Now in his 70s, Massino posed little threat of returning to a life of crime, especially considering that no Mafia crew would ever welcome him back. He had done a great deal in service of the government and prosecutors, and this was his reward. His health was also deteriorating at the time, a common cause for early release from prison, but Massino ended up surviving for another 10 years. He fell ill and died in late summer of 2023.

When acting boss Vincent Basciano was facing legal trouble between 2007 and 2011, he had chosen the younger Salvatore Montagna, the Canadian-born capo that owned a steel and iron manufactory in Brooklyn, to be the next acting boss in his stead. Montagna selected Nicky Santora, the capo who had taken over the late Sonny Black Napolitano's old crew, to be his underboss. Tony Rabito, an old-timer by the late-2000s, was selected to be his consigliere. Both Santora and Rabito had done time in prison as a result of FBI agent Joe Pistone's testimonies because they were directly implicated in the Donnie Brasco incident. With young leadership and a pair of veterans to back up the boss, the Bonanno

Family was starting to reform itself again. Despite Montagna's age, which otherwise could have allowed for a decades-long reign, he was not destined to be boss for long. With all the Bonanno made guys who had turned informant in recent years, it was only a matter of time before they dug up something on the steelmaker. In 2009, the hammer came down. Since Montagna was Canadian by birth and did not hold American citizenship, the U.S. government saw fit to simply expel him from the country. His immigration status was revoked, and he was deported back to Canada, eventually settling in Montreal, where he went on to make waves in the Rizzuto Family.

Meanwhile, the Rizzutos were dealing with problems that presented opportunities to the former boss-turned-deportee. Vito, Montreal's top crime lord at the time, had been implicated in 2004 in the murder of the three capos during the Red versus Black struggle in the '80s. Vito, of course, was one of the Canadians brought down to help with the ambush and execution. The boss was arrested that year and spent a great deal of resources trying to fight the Canadian governments attempts to extradite him to the US, as American prosecutors had requested. Because Canadian law prohibits the death penalty, they refused to extradite Vito as long as that was an option—prosecutors in Brooklyn eventually took capital punishment off the table to get Vito back to the country for trial, which they successfully did in 2006. Massino, one the men who arranged for Vito to come down to do the hit in the first place, had already flipped by now and was more than ready to testify against the Montreal don. Rizzuto, however, was eager to accept a plea deal and he did so before Massino got the chance. He received a large fine and 10 years in prison to be served at a penitentiary in Colorado. While Vito was out of the picture, Montagna tried to seize control over the Montreal underworld, but eventually ran afoul with some of the Rizzuto men. Montagna was murdered in 2011.

After Montagna was kicked out of the country, Vincent Badalamenti, the TV salesman and bagel-shop owner, allegedly became the new boss, at least in title. In early 2012, the new boss and Nicky Santora were both indicted. A few months later, Badalamenti pled guilty to loansharking charges and received a year and a half behind bars. Santora, for his part, pled guilty to extortion the next year and received a sentence about 2 months longer than Badalamenti's. Later in 2013, a bunch of other mafiosi in Santora's crew were pinched, many of them arrested while carrying illegal weaponry. The state of New York had them on loansharking, gambling (they allegedly ran a massive sports betting ring based out of Costa Rica), as well as narcotics charges. It was another bad couple of years for the Bonannos; the government of New York seized on the indictments as an opportunity to renew public support for the war against organized crime. They showcased the sheer number of gangsters arrested and the value of their international criminal enterprise as evidence that, perhaps, the Mafia was on the comeback in New York City. Cyrus Vance, the District Attorney for Manhattan, claimed that "the charges against this Bonanno crew and their captain, Nicholas Santora, make clear that traditional organized crime refuses to go away" (quoted in Scarpo, 2018). Since the 1980s, when the New York Mafia faced an onslaught of RICO charges that decimated nearly every single mob Family, many in the public believed that the Mafia was largely dead, a nonissue. Even the government started to treat them in a similar way in later years, as the national law enforcement shifted their focus away from organized crime to antiterrorism and homeland defense. However, 2013 was a grim reminder of their presence.

In 2013 Mike Mancuso, who was already in prison at the time, was selected as the new Bonanno don. He was about 7 years into a sentence of up to 15 years for the murder of Randy Pizzolo, an associate of the Bonanno Family. Tony Aiello, a soldier in the Family, was also indicted and had received twice the sentence that Mancuso did because he was allegedly the one who actually pulled the trigger on Pizzolo. After Mancuso was tapped for the job, he made Thomas "Tommy D" DiFiore his acting boss on the street. DiFiore was close to 70 at the time, but at least he wasn't in prison. Besides, Mafia Families for years had been promoting older members to top positions whenever they could, because in the event they got arrested, they typically received far lighter sentences than a young man would have. They typically had convincing health problems that their defense attorneys could use to argue for lenient sentences, so what may have been a decade for a young capo might turn into only a year or two for an old, ailing boss. DiFiore carried on the day-to-day Family activity until 2015, when he was indicted for using extortion tactics to collect the debt that was illegally owed to him (i.e., loansharking). He pled guilty and ended up receiving 21 months in prison and time served, meaning that he only had 7 months of his sentence left by the time he was convicted.

In DiFiore's absence, capo Joe Cammarano was the next acting boss. This, unfortunately, kicked off another power struggle within the remains of the Bonanno Family as the members split into two factions. The first were Mancuso loyalists; the other were those who favored Cammarano and wanted him to seize power fully from the still-imprisoned Mancuso. Cammarano was apparently not in favor of war, and instead wanted to be seen as having won power fairly and diplomatically. Believing he would have the support of a majority of capos, he took it to a vote to make it official and make him seem less treacherous. The diplomatic coup ultimately failed, though, and Mancuso retained the title of boss. A few years later, when Mancuso was released, one of his first orders was to "retire" Cammarano permanently for his behavior as acting boss. Cammarano was assaulted, but the hits were unsuccessful. Mancuso also allegedly put a contract out on Cammarano's brothers.

There was another major problem for the Family in the mid-2010s. In winter of 2017, a Bonanno capo named Damiano Zummo was arrested with several others in his crew and charged with narcotics distribution and firearm possession. Two years earlier, Zummo had flown up to Canada to conduct the induction ceremony of several new members of the Bonanno Family's Toronto faction. The ceremony took place in the Toronto-Hamilton area and was presided over by both American and Canadian mob leaders. Unfortunately for Zummo and the Bonannos, Enzo Morena was one of the men they were welcoming into their ranks that day. Unbeknownst to any of the made guys there, Morena was an informant and had been working with the government for more than three years. The entire induction ceremony, as well as countless hours of other conversations, were all recorded. If that wasn't bad enough, there was another imposter among the men who were made during that ceremony. He was an undercover police agent, and he had infiltrated the Family and actually became a soldier. It was Donnie Brasco all over again, except this time he actually got the chance to join the Family officially, and obtain both audio and even video recordings of the most secretive of Mafia traditions that dated back a century, at this point. It was all part of a joint US-Canadian operation into organized crime's role in narcotics and weapons trafficking, and the induction ceremony was the icing on the already successful cake. It was the same investigation that saw Zummo's indictment, and it also led to the arrest of two other members of Mafia royalty—Giuseppe and Domenico Violi, two sons of the once-illustrious Bonanno capo Paolo Violi of the bygone Cotroni Family.

In 2022, Mancuso had been out of prison for some time. That year, a funeral was held for Vito Grimaldi, a respected Bonanno capo who also happened to be the father-in-law of Joe Cammarano. Mancuso gave the disgraced former acting boss a direct warning not to show his face at the funeral, and a major scuffle ensued when he decided to attend anyway. With him were his brothers as well as a hired crew of thugs serving as a security team in case things went south. They were apparently members of a New York motorcycle gang. Mancuso's men faced off with Cammarano and his biker allies, and several on both sides ended up severely injured. After this is when Mancuso put orders out on the brothers as well, and they later had their homes shot up and their businesses wrecked and torched. They have allegedly been in hiding ever since.

CONCLUSION

The "glory" of the organization that the old Castellammarese boss Joe Bonanno implanted with his name is gone forever. The Family that once stood tall in New York City while their peers crumbled around them is now hobbled and staggering, a shell of its former self. The old rules and codes that used to keep mobsters from eating their own had all fallen to the wayside decades ago. Even guys like Joe Massino, who held on to their steadfast belief in the value of *omerta* well into the 1990s and beyond, had eventually realized the futility in sticking to old principles when the new generation disregards them completely. Friendships in the Mafia underworld only go so far as business allows. Cash always was the only thing that really mattered in that life, but the sense of mutual benefit and camaraderie was far stronger in the era of guys like Lucky Luciano, Vito Genovese, Tommy Lucchese, and Joe Bananas. Today, even the threat of a RICO charge is enough to convince many guys to flip.

Part of the reason for this state of affairs was American law enforcements decision to finally treat organized crime like a genuine threat to society. As police agencies became less corrupt and more difficult to bribe, so were the various Mafia Families inhabiting America's large cities made less effective. Compared to the 1990s and beyond, the era of bootleggers and victimless crimes of vice truly was the golden age for the American Mafia. Another main reason for the lack of integrity now seen by even the most hardened of mafiosi was the introduction of narcotics as a main source of income for the New York Families. Drugs acted like a poison for crews that got involved in their distribution, and although they promised a very large and very quick return on investment, they also seemed to virtually guarantee incredibly stiff criminal penalties. These were penalties that guys were desperate to avoid, especially those with a wife and children at home. Ratting out your closest friends essentially just became easier and easier, until it finally became the default option. The Mafia made spirited attempts to innovate alongside law enforcement and find new and fresh ways to counteract their tactics, but ultimately greed, gluttony, and selfishness was the cause of the Mafia's downfall, particularly the Bonanno Family. It's not entirely clear what will be next for the Bonannos or where they will find themselves in the history of the Mafia once all is said and done. However, it is clear that the Family is obviously still deeply fractured. Like all the other Families, they are still susceptible to destructive and dangerous egos, brutal and violent power grabs, and civil wars.

One wonders how the Family's course may have differed if Joe Bananas himself did not fall victim to his own greed back in the 1960s. He set his powerful Family on a path from which they never fully recovered, and their misfortune could convincingly be blamed on the Family's namesake himself. He was not directly responsible for what happened to the Family through the '80s, '90s, and beyond, but it was personalities like his that dragged the Mafia into the public attention. As much as the younger generation of mafiosi can be blamed for their lack of honor, it must be remembered who set these precedents in the first place. After all, Don Peppino willingly wrote a tell-all book in the '80s after he retired from Mafia life, a retirement that was a luxury not typically afforded to made guys. After that, it is a miracle that guys like Massino were able to cling to the outdated Mafia tenets at all. Despite the ultimately negative effect the original Family boss had on organized crime, no other Mafia Family in history is so closely defined by its relationship to a single man—Joe Bonanno. He remains the quintessential Mafia boss, one that evokes images of a simpler time in mob life where bosses ruled for decades and each one seemed to have the entire world in the palm of their hand.

REFERENCES

Amorusa, D. (2010 November 3). "Aftermath of a hit: The murder of three Bonanno captains." GangstersInc. https://gangstersinc.org/profiles/blogs/aftermath-of-a-hit-the-murder#google_vignette

DeStefano, A. (2008). *King of the Godfathers.* Kensington Books.

Faber, H. (1979 December 5). "Cheese company studied for organized crime tie." *New York Times.* https://www.nytimes.com/1979/12/05/archives/cheese-company-studied-for-organized-crime-tie-letter-to-joseph.html

Humphreys, A. (2017 November 9). "'Congratulations': Undercover agent inducted into mafia in secret ceremony captured on video by police." *National Post.* https://nationalpost.com/news/canada/congratulations-undercover-agent-inducted-into-mafia-in-secret-ceremony-in-canada-captured-on-video-by-police

Lamothe, L. & Humphreys, A. (2008). *The sixth family: The collapse of the New York mafia and the rise of Vito Rizzuto.* Mississauga: Wiley Books.

"'Last don' Joseph Massino convicted, faces prison time." (2004 July 31). *The Herald Times.*

Pistone, D. (1989). *Donnie Brasco: My undercover life in the mafia.* New York: Penguin Press.

Raab, S. (2005). *Five families: The rise, decline, and resurgence of America's most powerful mafia empires.* New York: Thomas Dunne Books.

Scarpo, E. (2014 December 1). "Bonanno's plan kept the peace in Canada's mafia." *CosaNostraNews.* https://www.cosanostranews.com/2014/12/bonannos-original-plan-kept-peace-in.html#google_vignette

Scarpo, E. (2016 March 12). "What mob boss Vito Rizzuto did when Joe Massino flipped." *CosaNostraNews.* https://www.cosanostranews.com/2016/02/what-vito-rizzuto-did-when-joe-massino.html

Scarpo, E. (2018 October 29). "Riches to rags to riches: Profile of longtime Bonanno mobster Nicky cigars Santora." *CosaNostraNews.* https://www.cosanostranews.com/2018/10/nicky-cigars-santora-historical-profile.html

Sitwell, B. (2020 April 29). "The real reason top mobsters didn't fight in World War II." WeAretheMighty. https://www.wearethemighty.com/mighty-history/mobsters-world-war-ii/

Printed in Great Britain
by Amazon